D0044135

The Director's Manual

The Director's Manual

A Framework for Board Governance

PETER C. BROWNING
WILLIAM L. SPARKS

WILEY

CONTENTS

ACKNOWLEDGMENTS

The authors would like to thank a number of colleagues, friends, and family members whose support and assistance made this effort possible. Our editor Mark Morrow's practiced and experienced hand kept us on track, providing critical insight, recommendations, and advice. Wanda Craig and Tamara Burrell assisted us in early drafts of the manuscript. Erika Weed helped in our research and social media efforts. We gratefully acknowledge the support of our business partners Dennis Whittaker, Allen Rogers, and, of course, Shannon McFayden. We are especially grateful for the advice, counsel, and support of Keith Eades. We appreciate the artistic talent of our graphic designer, Yeshua Perez. We would also like to thank Matt Davis at Wiley for his recommendations and patience, and especially for supporting this effort from the very beginning.

PETER C. BROWNING

I would like to thank my fellow directors with whom I have served and learned so much over the past twenty-six years and my teammates at the two companies in which I served as CEO, where we learned together the role of the board, its strengths, and its limitations.

If not for the urging of my partner and friend, Will Sparks, I am not sure this book would have ever gotten off the ground, so I offer my deepest appreciation to him for his strong support and confidence that we could produce a useful, relevant book that would be helpful to aspiring and current directors. Of course, I want to acknowledge the hard work and incredible effort of Pat Rogers with whom I have worked for over twenty years. She is the only person capable of reading and deciphering my handwriting.

And, finally, I would like to thank my wife Kathy for her continuing and unwavering support, encouragement, and love.

WILLIAM L. SPARKS

I would like to thank my family, friends, colleagues, and students who have inspired, challenged, and supported me over the years. Thanks to my colleagues at EnPro Industries, especially Steve Macadam, Ken Walker, Robert McLean, and Susan Sweeney, for their support and encouragement. I owe a debt of gratitude to my colleagues at Queens University of Charlotte as well, especially Pamela Davies and John Bennett. I very much appreciate the attention to detail of Linda Healy Vespa and Elizabeth Henderson, who helped shape my writing, and to the late Jerry B. Harvey, John L. Lobuts, and Dominic J. Monetta, who helped shape my thinking. I would like especially to thank my family for their unwavering support. Finally, and, most importantly, I owe more than a debt of gratitude to Peter Browning who has been a mentor, colleague, and dear friend over the years; you've taught me more than you'll ever know.

PREFACE

E ach corporate board has its own unique culture, created by the mix of directors, the personality and style of the CEO, and the culture of the company. Boards operate within this context to fulfill their fiduciary duties to shareholders while at the same time satisfying growing regulatory reporting requirements and regulations. It's a balancing act that is difficult at best.

The Director's Manual provides a proven, flexible framework to help boards of directors meet these challenging requirements while allowing each board to do so in the context of its own unique culture and business demands. The framework offered in this book provides guidance that is well suited for both established and new boards as they convene members and establish themselves within an organization.

Help is provided with regard to all aspects of board governance, including the role of the board, board schedules, dealing with a disruptive director, member selection, advice on management of group dynamics, and the creation of high-performing boards. Further guidance is contained in a comprehensive set of board and director assessments and a proprietary assessment (Board Culture Profile) that measures the most important determinant of board performance: group culture.[1]

WHY WE WROTE THIS BOOK

The impetus for writing the book was rooted in both our interest in, and our experience with, board governance, and the increasing scrutiny of shareholders and shareholder activists in board structure and performance. We believe this book will be an essential educational and practical resource for both current and aspiring directors, since it blends leadership and research findings on organizational dynamics with practical, straightforward advice for corporate directors, along with a solid set of how-to best practices.

Corporate boards are influenced by the prevailing corporate governance climate outside the boardroom. If the economy is booming, unemployment is low, and the country's confidence is high, then a board's set of priorities and options are likely to be very different from those in times of economic and social uncertainty.

Although this may seem to be an obvious connection, most resources concerned with board governance don't fully explore the impact of this symbiotic relationship between the world inside the corporate boardroom and the realities of the world outside the boardroom. And, even when the impact of this board and real-world relationship is covered in these resources, little practical advice and useful tools are offered.

The Director's Manual directly addresses this information shortfall by providing governance guidelines that are not only clear and concise but also immediately applicable to every board type and environment.

Chapter 1

THE CHANGING WORLD OF BOARD GOVERNANCE

How We Got Here

What's in This Chapter?
- How and Why Boards Have Changed
- A Barometer for CEO Compensation
- Why Pay Ratios Have Changed Radically
- A Board Governance Tipping Point
- Impact of the 2008 Financial Meltdown
- Chapter Summary and What's Next

One of the principle tenets of our consulting work is that every board is operationally and culturally unique. It is this simple fact that makes constructing a single, all-inclusive set of board governance best practices an impossible task. Therefore, the guidance in this book is not positioned as a set of "hard and fast" rules or universally applied "must have" characteristics. Rather, the guidance is based on a flexible framework approach that allows boards to meet their fiduciary and governance duties while remaining responsive to the real cultural dynamics that directly influence the quality and consistency of decision making.

A framework approach also has a second advantage: it allows boards to respond appropriately to an ever-changing external socio-economic and political landscape. This is an important point, since society's swiftly moving cultural currents, along with the ebb and flow of an economy's strength, has a profound impact on the performance expectations of corporate boards. Of course, this is no grand revelation to anyone reading this book, but we believe these concepts are important to keep in mind as context for the board governance recommendations made in the pages that follow.

HOW AND WHY BOARDS HAVE CHANGED

If you were asked to make a list of the most important game-changing events or trends that have profoundly impacted the U.S. economy and culture in the last sixty-five years, the list that you would make would likely include at least the following:

- A move away from a manufacturing economy to a service economy following decades of dominance in the post–Second World War global economy.
- Improvements in automation and the manufacturing process of the 1970s and 1980s. It was a trend that further undermined the manufacturing sector over the years as computer-driven machinery and tools (robotics, CAD-CAM design tools, etc.) replaced individual workers. Global competition also slowly eroded the U.S. manufacturing base as more and more man-ufacturing jobs moved to countries outside U.S. borders with lower labor costs.
- The diminishing influence and power of organized labor's ability to guarantee members a lifetime of a steady, living wage and a fully funded, secure pension upon retirement.
- The "creative destruction" of industries in the 1980s brought about by the world of leveraged buyouts and a ruthless cadre of "corporate raiders" who broke up many marquee old-line companies and sold off the divisions to score huge profits for themselves.

- The dot-com bubble that began its rise in the early 1990s and continued throughout the decade until it popped, to a devastating effect, in 2001. Investment strategy at the time was a race toward unrealistic valuation. Investors were willing to fund nearly any technological start-up venture even if it lacked a viable business plan. It is interesting to note that this investment setback did little to cloud the financial community's continued unrealistic economic outlook. In fact, this unsound enthusiasm in the marketplace was encouraged in large part by favorable economic policies of the federal government, supported by a period of low inflation due largely to lower cost of goods from China and a continuing worldwide technological revolution.

- The impact of blatant corporate malfeasance in 2001, exemplified by three highly visible corporations at the time: WorldCom, Enron, and Tyco. It was a revelation that rocked both the investment community and individual stockholders. Again, high-flying investors and shareholders lost millions of dollars when these companies declared bankruptcy (Enron Corporation declared bankruptcy in December of 2001), a singular action that further exposed an underbelly of lies and deceit that had pervaded these organizations at the very top and eventually put thousands of ordinary workers out on the street without jobs or their life savings.

- Finally, the 2008 huge financial meltdown and the economic panic that followed. It was a time of fear and shock as we watched once powerful brokerage houses as well as large banks and old-line industrial giants teeter on the brink of declaring bankruptcy. It took massive, last-minute, stopgap federal cash infusions to save the world's economy and to shore up institutions that were deemed "too big to fail."

WHY THESE EVENTS ARE IMPORTANT

The reason for noting these historical and societal events is twofold. First, it demonstrates how past events impact the current expectations placed on corporate boards; and second, it establishes the contextual "waters" for the operational strategies, policies, and

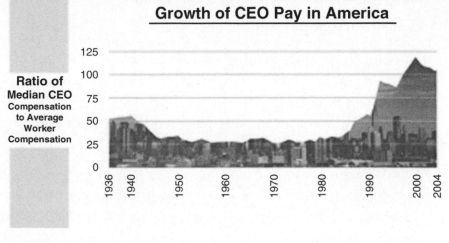

Figure 1.1   History of CEO Pay

Source: Peter Browning Partners

procedures that most boards follow today. This chapter will focus on two specific trends that grew out of these economic and social gyrations:

- Ever-increasing chief executive officer (CEO) compensation (see Figure 1.1).
- The impact of a 2002 change to the New York Stock Exchange (NYSE) Listed Company Manual that required "non-management directors to meet at regularly scheduled executive sessions without management." While this change to the NYSE Listed Company Manual (303A.03) occurred during the same time period as the passage of the 2002 Sarbanes-Oxley Act (Congress's response to public outrage over Enron's corporate malfeasance and greed), the fact that the two actions occurred at the same time is a coincidence of timing. The fact is, as important as the Sarbanes-Oxley legislation has been to curbing illegal corporate activities, we would argue that the NYSE Listed Company Manual change has ultimately produced the most far-reaching impact on board governance, performance, and effectiveness.

A BAROMETER FOR CEO COMPENSATION

According to Carola Frydman and Raven E. Saks, authors of "Historical Trends in Executive Compensation 1936–2003," CEO compensation experienced three distinct phases over the last seventy-five years: World War II, the mid-1940s to the 1970s, and the 1980s through the 1990s.[1]

Prior to World War II, the median executive compensation was about fifty-six times higher than average wages, although CEO compensation did decline sharply during World War II. After the war the U.S. economy experienced a period of unfettered growth and development. This expansion created a rapidly growing middle class that was confident about lifelong careers with the same company, steadily rising wages, and opportunities for career advancement. All of this confidence brought with it a predictable stream of disposable cash to buy American products.

Interestingly, executive salaries during this period of expansion remained relatively low and, in fact, slowly fell until 1970, when they reached a low point of twenty-five times average wages. During this period organizations promoted their most senior and capable executives to the CEO spot and then compensated them with a salary, cash bonuses, and limited stock options. As a rule, these groomed CEOs kept their jobs until retirement.

Global Competition Brings Change

Global competition in the 1970s imposed new economic pressures on corporate America. Nations previously ravaged by war, especially Japan, took full advantage of industrial redevelopment support from the United States. Soon these countries began to compete directly with their benefactor, especially in the car and consumer electronics markets. This competition resulted in the closing of many U.S. manufacturing plants, and once thriving towns, cities, and communities, and even whole regions, were economically decimated. All of this upheaval and uncertainty in the manufacturing sector from mid-1970 to the end of the 1980s resulted in a 2,000 percent increase in merger and acquisition activity (as compared to previous years) as companies struggled to keep control of their organizations and to avoid the ravages of a hostile corporate takeover (Gladwell, 2009).[2]

The Impact of Strategic Planning

Beginning in the early 1980s, CEO compensation policy began to radically change as U.S. corporations switched their focus to long-term strategic planning models and away from more traditional, short-term business planning approaches. This was a change in thinking that directly impacted corporate board management and its priorities.

A key proponent of this long-term strategic planning approach was Bruce Doolin Henderson, who in 1963 founded the Boston Consulting Group. Corporate leaders, including General Electric's CEO Jack Welch, became disciples of the approach in the early 1980s, as did many university business schools and scores of consultants who were eager for the business opportunity created by Henderson's ideas.

In his 2010 book, *The Lords of Strategy: The Secret Intellectual History of the New Corporate World,* which is about Henderson's influence on business practices worldwide, author Walter Kiechel notes that Henderson literally "changed the world." "Few people," Kiechel says, "have had as much impact on international business in the second half of the twentieth century." (A complete account of this industry-changing consulting group can be found in *The Lords of Strategy: The Secret Intellectual History of the New Corporate World.*)[3]

The Impact of Long-Term Incentives

The shift to corporate strategic-planning practices not only created a multibillion-dollar consulting industry but also set the groundwork for a new way to compensate CEOs and other top corporate executives. Now, instead of traditional compensation packages (i.e., salary, cash bonuses, and limited stock options), corporate boards had a range of pay strategies that mirrored these emerging long-term business planning strategies. CEO pay packages soon included long-term incentives (LTI) that tied a CEO's overall pay to the long-term performance of the company (typically, three years).

These changes to the traditional rubric used to calculate CEO compensation occurred just as investors and other financial community movers and shakers began to demand that companies produce higher profits within ever-shorter time lines. The pressure behind these short-term profit demands resulted in great measure from the dissolution of traditional pension plans and the significant expansion of mutual funds. These various funds competed with one another for shorter-term performance increases.

According to a recent article in *Foreign Affairs* magazine by Jerry Z. Muller, a history professor at The Catholic University of America, the hypercompetitive 1980s resulted in "companies (as well as various public-sector organizations) attempt[ing] to shift the risk by putting their pension funds into the hands of professional money managers, who were expected to generate significant profits." The result of this strategy, according to Muller, was that "retirement income for employees [was] now depend[ent] . . . on the fate of [the employee's] pension funds. "The change had the practical result of putting even more "pressure on corporate executives to produce short-term performance results."[4]

The shorter time line to increase profits also had an unfortunate downside: it created a temptation among fund managers, corporate CEOs, and others at the corporate top to boost immediate profits at the expense of longer-term investments, such as research and development or improving workforce skills.

Phase Three—The Results of Uncertainty

The final phase of Frydman and Saks's executive compensation development framework extended through the 1990s. It was a time when many CEOs lost their jobs because the company's promised performance failed to square with the company's earnings reality or because of increased merger and acquisition activity. The employment uncertainty led boards to offer highly sought after CEOs and their teams a "change of control agreement" (also known as a "golden parachute") in their employment contracts. This practice grew to such a degree that the Internal Revenue Service (IRS) responded in 1984 with new rules that capped these payments at

2.99 times the average of the last five Form 1099 income filings by the CEOs. Any income in excess of this amount would now be subject to a nondeductible 20 percent excise tax.[5]

By the late 1980s, companies began offering stock options (LTIs) stock options in lieu of cash for LTI payments as public sentiment (and pressure) believed these rewards would be more aligned with shareholder value.

Soon, the stock benefit alone began to make up almost half of high-level managerial pay (Frydman and Saks, 2007), a state of affairs that only served to increase the CEO/worker wage gap as stock values soared during the period's bull market. As noted even in Graef Crystal's 1991 book, *In Search of Excess: The Overcompensation of American Executives*, the preceding twenty years had seen CEO pay increase by more than 400 percent while the typical American worker's wages remained stagnant.[6]

In 1993, in response to investor complaints, Congress enacted Internal Revenue Code Section 162(m), which caps a public company's corporate income tax deduction at $1 million per year for each of its top executives. The provision did, however, include an important exception in the case of preapproved, performance-based compensation plans, a "loophole" that allowed the continued growth of long-term executive pay and bonuses. Clearly, this was not the original law's intention. Nor was it the lawmaker's intention to allow the value of stock option grants to CEOs of the S&P 500 firms to leap by 45 percent on average (during the law's first year in effect) and then to nearly double over the next two years. As the chairman of the Securities and Exchange Commission (SEC), Christopher Cox noted in an article by Mark Maremont and Charles Forelle in the December 27, 2006 edition of the *Wall Street Journal*, that the 1993 law "deserves pride of place in the Museum of Unintended Consequences."[7]

Even the end of the great 1990s dot-com bubble did nothing to slow the rise of executive compensation. By 2005 the gap between executives and workers expanded even further, and by 2005 an executive in our study earned 110 times an average worker's earnings—about twice the corresponding ratio prior to World War II. Due to the generous use of stock options as compensation, some top executives would eventually earn more than 700 times the pay of an average worker (Frydman and Saks, 2007).[8]

2002 — A BOARD GOVERNANCE TIPPING POINT

Interestingly, a pivotal change in board governance occurred during the market upheaval of the post-dot-com era. In 2001 employees at communications firm WorldCom, electronics and home security company Tyco, and energy giant Enron Corporation all were caught up in an episode of unparalleled corporate malfeasance. Enron's criminality was particularly egregious in the behavior of employees of certain prominent business partners — in particular, employees of the Chicago-based accounting firm, Arthur Andersen. At the time Arthur Andersen was one of the five largest audit and accountancy partnerships in the world.

Despite a one-hundred-year record of service and its business community prestige, the "Enron scandal" destroyed the venerable accounting firm. Arthur Andersen lost its Certified Public Accountant license in 2002 and quickly disappeared from the scene. Enron filed for bankruptcy in 2001, and many of its top executives were charged, convicted, and served prison time for their role in the scandal.

The fallout from these highly publicized events was a great deal of public and private scrutiny on boards of directors serving in publicly traded companies. In 2002 Congress enacted a new law, Sarbanes-Oxley (also known as the Corporate and Auditing Accountability and Responsibility Act), designed to address future corporate accounting integrity breaches.

KEY PROVISIONS OF THE SARBANES-OXLEY ACT

Each of the eleven titles (or sections) of the Sarbanes-Oxley Act (SOX) mandates specific financial reporting requirements that

(continued)

(continued)

are intended to curb financial fraud and to increase financial reporting transparency.

SOX legislation was a direct response to revelations in the early 2000s of accounting fraud that was perpetrated by Enron, Tyco, and WorldCom.

Five of the eleven Sarbanes-Oxley provisions are associated with major points that we make in this book, including the following:

- Section 320 focuses on statutory reports to include certifications.
- Section 401 focuses on the accuracy of financial statements.
- Section 404 is associated with the adequacy of internal control structure and procedures.
- Section 409 concerns public disclosure of significant changes in a company's financial condition.
- Section 802 outlines penalties for destroying or falsifying records to obstruct or impede an investigation.

The law's intent was to strengthen the integrity of internal reporting by requiring top management to personally certify the accuracy of key financial information and by imposing severe penalties for fraudulent activity. The Sarbanes-Oxley Act also increased the independence of the outside auditors who review the accuracy of corporate financial statements and increased the oversight role of boards of directors.

The Most Impactful Governance Change

While some would suggest that our current board governance environment is a result of the Sarbanes-Oxley Act, that assertion would be only partially true. Certainly, the Sarbanes-Oxley Act has had a profound impact on the internal reporting requirements of corporations. In particular, there are five key sections of the legislation that are associated with the major points that we make in this book. The first is Section 320, which is focused on statutory reports to include certifications; the second, Section 401, is focused on the accuracy of financial statements published by issuers and requires that they be presented in a manner that does not contain incorrect statements or admit to stating material information. The third, Section 404, is concerned with requirements for issuers to publish information in their annual reports concerning the scope and adequacy of internal control structure and procedures. The fourth section, Section 409, requires issuers to disclose to the public, on an urgent basis, information on material changes in their financial condition or operations. Finally, Section 802 is a provision that imposes penalties or fines and/or up to twenty years' imprisonment for altering, destroying, mutilating, concealing, and falsifying records to obstruct or impede an investigation.

However, the pivotal change that would forever change the landscape of corporate boards took place on August 1, 2002. That's when the NYSE Board of Directors approved and submitted to the SEC for approval a revision to their Listed Company Manual that recommended, among others, the following corporate board guidelines:

- A majority of corporate board members must be independent; that is, they cannot have any material interest in the corporation.
- Independent directors are the only voting members of the board.
- Boards must have a minimum of three standing committees: audit, compensation, and governance/nominating.
- Boards must conducting annual assessments of the CEO, the board itself, and each of the three standing committees.
- Independent directors must meet periodically in executive session without company management being present.

Of all the Listed Company Manual changes approved by the NYSE, the last one requiring the independent directors to meet without the CEO represents a sea change in the world of board governance. Prior to this change, CEOs never would have allowed this meeting to take place, and with good reason; you never knew what might be discussed in the meeting, including a CEO's performance and compensation. We discuss this important change in more detail in Chapter 3, "Key Board Leadership Roles," along with the many implications that this change has had on board governance activities.

Other Important Governance Changes

Another important change to the world of board governance occurred in April 2003, when the SEC implemented rule 30b1–4 that required registered management investment companies to disclose their proxy voting policies and voting records. Although this ruling might appear to be fairly straightforward, the practical impact of implementing it certainly was not. At the time of the ruling, mutual funds represented 18 percent of all publically traded U.S. corporate equity (about $2 trillion of value). Suddenly, those who managed these large funds were required to vote on every proxy matter. This meant that the managers would have to understand hundreds, if not thousands, of proxy votes and cast votes appropriately.

The solution to this dilemma was essentially to outsource this work to proxy advisory firms, principally to Institutional Shareholder Services (ISS), a firm founded in 1985 by shareholder activists Robert Monks and Neil Minnow. The purpose of ISS originally had been to promote good governance and to raise the level of active and informed proxy voting among institutional investors. However, by 2006 opinions about ISS on proxy votes began to have considerable influence on the final outcomes of proxy voting. A 2006 article by Robert D. Hershey Jr. in the New York Times, titled "A Little Industry with a Lot of Sway on Proxy Votes," provided good evidence of this influence. The article noted that by the firm's own estimate ISS opinions affect the governance decisions of a cadre of professional investor's controlling $25 trillion in assets, a figure that encompasses half the value of the world's common stocks.[9] As aptly characterized by David W. Smith, president of the Society of Corporate Secretaries and Governance Professionals, "the influence these advisors wield is extraordinary."[10]

KEY PROVISIONS OF THE DODD-FRANK ACT

Dodd-Frank (or The Dodd-Frank Wall Street Reform and Consumer Protection Act) was passed by the Obama administration in 2010 in response to the 2008 financial crisis. It is a complex piece of legislation that is intended to prevent the particular set of circumstances that nearly crashed the world economy in 2008.

The act covers sixteen major areas of reform, ranging from consumer protection, to preventing abusive lending and mortgage practices by banks, to ensuring that financial institutions will never again be "too big to fail."

Dodd-Frank, named after its sponsors, Senator Christopher J. Dodd (D-CT) and U.S. Representative Barney Frank (D-MA), also created various councils and oversight agencies that are charged with ensuring that the aims of the legislation are realized. Since these mechanisms are complex and often controversial, many of them are still being implemented. Here are some of the major provisions of the legislation:

- Creation of the Financial Stability Oversight Council (FSOC) to monitor the overall risks in the financial industry (including hedge funds). The council's members include the Federal Reserve, the SEC, and a newly formed agency called the Consumer Financial Protection Bureau (CFPB) that is intended to protect consumers from "unscrupulous" business practices by banks.
- Dodd-Frank also mandated that the riskiest of investment instruments, such as credit default swaps, be regulated by the SEC or the Commodity Futures Trading Commission (CFTC). Insurance companies were also targeted by the legislation, and a new Federal Insurance Office (FIO) was set up to determine if the largest of these companies might be a potential risk to the system. Insurance underwriter AIG

(*continued*)

(continued)

needed an $85 billion federal bailout to stay in business in 2008.

- An Office of Credit Rating was created at the SEC to ensure that credit ratings agencies such as Moody's and Standard & Poor's do a better job of monitoring and recommending investment tools.

On June 30, 2014, the SEC, responding to a rising chorus of complaints about the outsized influence of ISS and other proxy voting entities such as Glass Lewis, published a ruling entitled "Proxy Voting: Proxy Voting Responsibilities of Investment Advisers and Availability of Exemptions from the Proxy Rules for Proxy Advisory Firms." Specifically, the ruling noted that "the proxy Voting Rule does not require that investment advisers and clients agree that the investment adviser will undertake all of the proxy voting responsibilities."[11]

The ruling has pushed large institutional investors to develop their own capabilities for the determination of what votes to cast on a particular proxy matter. For example, BlackRock, the largest manager of money, just recently published its own 2015 proxy voting guide.

IMPACT OF THE 2008 FINANCIAL MELTDOWN

The financial crisis of 2007–2008 was the worst financial crisis since the Great Depression in 1929, and it threatened to completely collapse the American banking system. In large measure the collapse was caused by a housing bubble that peaked in 2006 as a complex system of subprime mortgages and questionable trading practices was revealed and the whole house of cards quickly crumbled.

One of the most notable events was the failure of Lehman Brothers. Before declaring bankruptcy in 2008, Lehman Brothers was the fourth largest investment bank in the United States. A court-appointed examiner later found that the bank had moved $50 billion of bad investments off its balance sheet each quarter to hide its actual financial condition. Like the Enron scandal, Lehman Brothers' fall was seen by stockholders as another example of corporate America's failure to monitor itself.

As if the country needed another example of financial malfeasance, the Bernie Madoff scandal also surfaced in 2008. Madoff was the founder of a Wall Street investment firm, Bernard L. Madoff Investment Securities. Madoff eventually admitted that his Ponzi scheme had defrauded thousands of individual and institutional investors out of more than $64 billion. Madoff is now serving a 150-year prison sentence for his crimes.

Federal Bailout

As a result of these scandals and associated regulatory failures, the economy spiraled dangerously toward economic depression, and trust in the stock market and in big business plummeted as quickly as unemployment rose. Finally, the U.S. government played the only hand that it had in the game and pumped more than $750 billion into the largest "too big to fail" financial institutions through the Troubled Asset Relief Program (TARP). The government also loaned about $110 billion to the auto industry to keep it afloat, with a majority of the relief going to General Motors and Chrysler.

Multiple factors contributed to the 2008 financial crisis. The U.S. Senate's Levin–Coburn Report, the product of a two-year bipartisan investigation by the U.S. Senate Permanent Subcommittee on Investigations into the origins of the 2008 financial crisis, noted that the crisis was the result of "high risk, complex financial products; undisclosed conflicts of interest; the failure of regulators, the credit rating agencies, and the market itself to rein in the excesses of Wall Street." Others would argue that the 2008 financial crisis was another example of corporate greed and a failure of corporate boards to control excessive executive compensation.

While there might be debate about the causes of the financial crisis, the Dodd-Frank Act (named after Senator Christopher Dodd and U.S. Representative Barney Frank), which was signed into federal law by President Barack Obama in July 2010, was very clear about the legislation's intention in its preamble. The act states that its purpose is to "promote the financial stability of the United States by improving accountability and transparency in the financial system, to end 'too big to fail,' to protect the American taxpayer by ending bailouts, to protect consumers from abusive financial services practices, and for other purposes."

The Dodd-Frank legislation brought about the most significant changes to financial regulation since the financial reforms enacted following the Great Depression. In addition to curbs on the types of trading activities that financial institutions would be allowed to practice, the legislation gave additional powers to shareholders. The changes represented a seismic shift in this fundamental relationship. Among other provisions, the SEC was asked to grant shareholders the right to provide a nonbinding advisory vote, a "say on pay" for executive compensation.

Although the vote is not binding, directors are now required to regularly (annually, biannually, or triennially) submit to shareholders an advisory vote on the prior year compensation for the NEOs (named executive officers). If the affirming vote is less than 70 percent, then it may indicate that a problem exists in the correlation between the CEO's pay and the Total Shareholder Return (TSR) ratio of the company. This score is also a metric that ISS and other proxy services track and use in their evaluation of individual companies. Although the number of negative votes remains quite low, it does keep attention focused on this issue.

The other significant outcome from the Dodd-Frank Act is just beginning to unfold. The legislation called for changes aimed at better shareholder access. Specifically, it asked for a process to provide shareholders the ability to place candidates beyond those proposed by the board on the company's annual proxy list of candidates.

Although the regulation proffered by the SEC was contested and eventually dropped, no resolution is at hand. Shareholders are still asking for such a proviso to be placed on the proxy list for a shareholders' vote. Some companies, such as GE and Bank of America (among others), changed their bylaws to add this feature while others are dealing with it in their annual meeting. For example, the May 18,

2015 issue of the corporate board publication *Agenda* noted that "the most popular shareholder proposal topic this year has been proxy access, increasing fourfold from last year."[12]

CHAPTER SUMMARY

This chapter supports the board governance recommendations that we make later in this book by highlighting the major social, economic regulatory changes that contribute to today's board culture and practices. Specifically, this chapter makes the following key points.

CEO compensation continues to increase, despite increasing public attention to the gap between average worker and CEO compensation. This wage gap has increased from a low of twenty-five times that of an average wages to many multiples of that ratio, although the average gap generally caps at about 350 percent that of an average worker's wages in the company.

Clearly, this is an issue that will not disappear anytime soon. At the same time, the emphasis on pay for performance is showing results. In May 2009 *Forbes* published an article by Emily Lambert titled "The Right Way to Pay," highlighting a move toward "pay packages that reward long term performance rather than short term greed." Importantly, 3,422 companies held "say on pay votes" in 2014, in which only 66 companies failed (1.9 percent).[13]

As a May 17, 2015 article, "It's (Still) Their Party," by David Gelles in the *New York Times* said about this issue on their annual survey of CEO compensation, "this apparent satisfaction with pay may be a result of the rising stock market. Shareholder dissent, when it does crop up, typically occurs at companies that have awarded lush compensation even as their performance has lagged. Investors watching their shares go up are less likely to be outraged by a sizeable bonus or stuck grant."[14]

Although the most visible legislative result of the "Enron scandal" is the Sarbanes-Oxley Act, aimed at the accounting abuses at the root of Enron's corporate malfeasance, the most important rule change impacting board governance occurred in 2002, when the NYSE Board of Directors approved and submitted to the SEC for approval a revision to their Listed Company Manual, recommending that independent directors must meet periodically in executive session without company management being present.

Of all the Listing Company Manual changes approved by the NYSE, this is the most important action taken, and it represents a sea change in the world of board governance.

The Dodd-Frank Act is a consumer protection act signed into federal law by President Barack Obama in July 2010, which restricts the types of trading activities that financial institutions are allowed to practice. The law was enacted in response to the 2008 financial meltdown that nearly sent the United States and the world into a 1929-type depression. The Dodd-Frank legislation, among other consumer protections, gave shareholders the right to provide a nonbinding advisory vote, or a "say on pay," for executive compensation.

WHAT'S NEXT?

Chapter 2, "Role of the Board," offers some guiding principles for effective board governance. The chapter uses the story of the rise and fall of former Home Depot CEO Bob Nardelli to illustrate a cautionary tale for boards considering going outside the company to hire their next CEO. The story also supports two key principles: first, boards do not run companies; second, there are serious consequences in making the wrong choice of a CEO, and there is transformative power in making the right choice of a CEO.

Chapter 2

ROLE OF THE BOARD

What's in This Chapter?
- Home Depot's Leadership Question
- Two Key Guiding Principles
- Why Boards Exist
- Three Critical Questions That Boards Ask:
  - Does the Company Have the Right CEO?
  - Is a Robust Succession Plan in Place?
  - Is the Company Following the Right Strategy?
- Chapter Summary and What's Next

The Home Depot, the ubiquitous DYI (Do It Yourself) retailer, opened its first two cavernous 60,000-foot warehouse stores in Atlanta, Georgia, in June of 1979. At the time the concept of a one-stop home improvement store that focused on helping home project warriors refurbish bathrooms, replace doors and windows, build toolsheds, and complete a thousand other DYI projects clearly filled a marketplace niche. By 1989 the company had opened its 100th store, and by 1984 the company was listed as a publically traded company on the New York Stock Exchange (HD).

From the beginning, company founders Bernie Marcus and Arthur Blank credited Home Depot's success on a focus on superior customer service provided by trained and knowledgeable associates who are able to offer on-the-spot assistance for almost any home project. This people-focused philosophy was at the center of the vision that Home Depot's founding team had for the company, which also included investment banker Ken Langone and merchandising star Pat Farrah.

Throughout the 1980s and 1990s, the company grew at a brisk pace, making strategic acquisitions along the way. In 1994 Home Depot acquired Aikenhead's, a chain of Canadian home improvement centers, and in 2001 it acquired Total HOME, a Mexico-based home improvement center. In 2006 Home Depot extended its reach into the international market with the acquisition of the Chinese home improvement chain, The Home Way.[1]

HOME DEPOT'S LEADERSHIP QUESTION

In 2000 Bernie Marcus announced that he would retire as the head of the company that he had cofounded, ending a successful twenty-one-year tenure. The assumption had always been that Arthur Blank, the other cofounder, would succeed Marcus as CEO. However, due to a unique set of circumstances, The Home Depot board was presented with what they saw as a great opportunity to select a new high-profile leader from outside the company. As it turned out, this "opportunity" to bring in a CEO from outside the company did not live up to the board's expectations.

Home Depot's leadership transition just happened to coincide with the announcement by General Electric (GE) that Jack Welch, perhaps one of the most famous CEOs in the world, was also retiring. Three high-level executives at GE were waiting in the wings; all were hoping to be chosen for the position of CEO by GE's board. The candidates included Bob Nardelli, Jim McNerney, and Jeff Immelt. Eventually, the board chose Jeff Immelt to replace Welch; that left two other candidates, McNerney and Nardelli, free to make other career plans. McNerney moved on to become CEO of 3M Company and then eventually took the top leadership position at Boeing, the Seattle-based aircraft manufacturer. Bob Nardelli accepted Home Depot's offer to replace the retiring Marcus.

Poor Choices by Chairman

Unfortunately, as good as his credentials and his potential for success were, Nardelli's selection proved to be a poor choice. First, the new leader was given a controversial set of guaranteed bonuses and other out-of-market compensation options that never sat well with the company's investors and shareholders. Nardelli was also given a powerful title: Chairman, President, and CEO of The Home Depot. The compensation package and inherent power vested in Nardelli's titles soon resulted in a considerable downward trend for the company.

A Change of Direction

Instead of continuing the company's customer-driven focus that had kept Home Depot's DYI customers loyal over the years, Nardelli chose a strategy that was focused on building market dominance in the wholesale building supply business. Nardelli initiated a series of large acquisitions, in this field aggressively acquiring an number of firms in this market. These acquisitions added significant debt to the balance sheet at a time when stiff competition, particularly from Lowe's, was chipping away at Home Depot's market advantage.

In addition, Nardelli's numbers-driven approach and confrontational, disruptive management style did not wear well with Home Depot's employees. Soon, these internal cultural problems trickled down to the customer level and ultimately showed up on the company's balance sheet as declining sales performance.

Share Price Drop

The Home Depot's stock price also reflected the impact of Nardelli's decisions. When Nardelli took over as CEO, the stock share price was $48.20 (January 2, 2001); when Nardelli departed the company in June of 2007, the stock price was $39.21. When this fall in share value is placed against the backdrop of a Dow Jones Industrial Average that grew from 10,887 to 13,688 during Nardelli's tenure, this indeed is a poor performance record. The continuation of Nardelli's extraordinarily generous compensation package just further angered the company's investors and shareholders.

In May of 2006, Nardelli made a huge tone-deaf decision in spite of the windstorm of investor and press criticism that was swirling around him at the time. Inexplicably, he moved the annual shareholder meeting from its home base in Georgia to the state of Delaware. Then, as if he were trying to add insult to injury, he requested that the company's board of directors not attend the meeting. This singularly poor example of board governance had very predictable results inside and outside the boardroom.

CNN Money.com put the controversy front and center in a May 26, 2006 article under the headline, "Shareholders to Home Depot Chief: You're Chicken." The headline referred to an angry shareholder who got up at this relocated board meeting and told Nardelli point-blank, "You hide behind the various metrics, you won't report same store sales, you're chicken." The board also got its share of vitriol from this unhappy shareholder. "This is outrageous that they (the board) are not willing to appear before shareholders," the shareholder said; ". . . I think they're too chicken to face shareholders, whether to allow a vote on CEO compensation or answer questions about the performance of the company."[2]

The denouement to this story was not long in coming. In February of 2007, Relational Investors, one of Home Depot's most significant investors, reached an agreement with the board to finally take decisive action. On February 22, 2007, David Batchelder, the founder of Relational Investors, joined the board. Four months later, in June of 2007, the company announced Nardelli's departure. In 2008 four of the then current directors involved in the original hiring of Nardelli were asked to leave the board.

TWO KEY GUIDING PRINCIPLES

The rise and fall of Bob Nardelli is on one hand a cautionary tale for boards, because it highlights the risks of going outside the company to hire the next CEO. The Nardelli story also illustrates two critical governance principles that will be covered in this chapter.

- The board cannot run the company, even if it desires to do so. The board's principle responsibility is to ensure that the right

CEO is in place. Regardless of the size of the company, the wrong CEO, in the wrong place and at the wrong time, can change the course of an enterprise in a very short period of time, as was illustrated by the Home Depot saga.

- On the other hand, Home Depot's leadership experience also illustrates what can happen when the board chooses the right CEO. After dismissing Nardelli, the board chose Frank Blake as Nardelli's successor. He was the former GE General Counsel whom Nardelli had brought with him to Home Depot. Although Blake had no experience in the retail environment, the new CEO thoughtfully and calmly settled the company. He returned the cultural climate to an even keel and again focused the company on customer service. Store results soon confirmed that Blake was on the right track as Home Depot returned to its focus on the DYI customer and service. Blake recently retired, receiving great accolades from inside and outside the company.

WHY BOARDS EXIST

In a March 2013 speech given during a Kellogg School of Management/ Aspen Institute Business and Society Conference, Aspen Institute Chairman David Langstaff noted that "the role of the board is to ensure that purpose, vision and core values are in place, and thus to give the CEO and the executive team the time and space to act responsibly." Langstaff went on to say that "boards must also help CEOs counter the short-term presence of the market, and ensure that companies do not make short-term accommodating decisions that are not in its long-term interest as responsible contributors to society."[3]

In slightly less precise but clear terms, boards exist principally to watch over the fiduciary interests of a company's shareholders and other interested stakeholders. It's a responsibility that extends to the widest range of stakeholders, including individual stockholders and those who manage mutual funds and/or those who select stocks based on a company's performance. This second group includes fund managers for universities and other public entities, as well as unions and all other groups that tie current and future pension payouts to the financial strength of a company.

The view that boards do not operate as a homogenous voting block that is concerned only with share price was echoed in March 2015 in the Schumpeter weekly column of the *Economist*, titled "The Business of Business."

> For decades, conservatives and progressives have argued over whether the purpose of a company is to maximize shareholder value or pursue boards' social needs. . . . In practice, of course, shareholders are often not a homogeneous block with a collective interest: Traders who buy on the whiff of a bid may have a different perspective from investors who have held shares for decades. Open-endedness reflects the reality of corporate life. Far from being slaves to the share price as progressives imagine most companies are engaged in a constant process of negotiation between managers and investors over other strategy and time horizons.[4]

Laurence D. Fink, Chairman and CEO of BlackRock, the largest manager of money in the world, echoed this point of view in a March 31, 2015 letter to five hundred of the largest companies in the United States: "It is critical, however, to understand that corporate leaders' duty of care and loyalty is not to every investor or trade who owns the companies' share at any moment in time, but to the company and its long-term owners."[5]

THREE CRITICAL QUESTIONS THAT BOARDS ASK

Whether the board meets once a month or, more typically, four to five times a year, a board is never actively engaged with the daily operations of a company. That's why the catch phrase, "noses in, fingers out," is such an appropriate rubric to explain the work of corporate boards. Boards have a clearly defined advisory role. It is the CEO (along with the CEO's management team) who ultimately must run the company responsibly. Still, boards play an essential role in helping a company's leadership achieve both the company's strategic goals and meeting shareholder expectations.

In many ways the principal value that board members offer is their collective wisdom to help companies answer three critical questions:

1. Is the right CEO running the company? This is not a single event, but part of a continuous evaluation process.
2. Does the company have a robust succession process, and does the plan include the appointment of a strong short-term successor for the business?
3. Does the company have the right strategy? If so, is that strategy being implemented effectively?

IS THE RIGHT CEO RUNNING THE COMPANY?

Boards play a vital role in choosing a leader who is able to influence others to follow. William Shakespeare tapped this essential leadership capacity in the play *Henry IV, Part I* when Glendower boasts, "I can call spirits from the vasty deep," to which Hotspur replies, "Why so can I, or so any man, but will they come when you do call for them?"[6]

Of course, finding the illusory "right leader" is no easy task, even if a potential CEO meets every criterion for past financial performance and experience levels, and even if that individual's values and leadership style perfectly fit with the organization's culture. The fact is, even if the perfectly aligned CEO has been chosen, failure is still possible. It's a story as old as recorded history.

Greek historian Plutarch more than two thousand years ago found that the right person in the right place at the right time makes all the difference. The truth is simply this: some individuals just have a way of overcoming obstacles and difficulties that stymied their predecessors and can reach goals that previous leaders were unable to reach.

As the management consultant, educator, and author Peter F. Drucker once said,

> *An effective executive does not need to be a leader in the sense that is now most commonly used. Harry Truman did not have an ounce of charisma. Some of the best business and nonprofit*

CEOs I've worked with over a 65 year consulting career were not stereotypical leaders. They were all over the map in terms of their personalities, attributes, values, strengths, and weaknesses. They range from extroverted to nearly reclusive, from easy-going to controlling, from generous to parsimonious.[7]

Predicting Leader Success Is Impossible

In the end the only way to tell if a right leadership choice has been made is to observe the job performance of the candidate. As Matthew J. Paese, vice president of executive solutions at Development Dimensions International (DDI), positioned this dilemma: "I am still waiting for the true realist to emerge from the board and announce, 'We are making this CEO succession decision recognizing that it probably won't work out and that next year at this time we will be looking for a replacement.'"[8] Of course, it is absurd to imagine any board openly stating the expected failure of an incoming CEO, but from a purely statistical point of view, it's not an outrageous statement. In fact, over the last decade, CEO turnover has increased by more than 50 percent and performance-related departures have increased by more than 300 percent.

The Cost of a Wrong Choice

The price for failed leadership at the CEO level is almost incalculable, regardless of whether the candidate is internally developed or hired from the outside. The saga of Bob Nardelli's tenure as CEO of Home Depot is an instructive example. Another well-known example of the cost of hiring the wrong CEO is Hewlett-Packard's story of unfortunate leadership decisions that it made beginning in the late 1990s.

In David F. Larcker and Brian Tayan's 2011 article for the *Stanford Closer Look Series*, "Leadership Challenges at Hewlett-Packard (HP): Through the Looking Glass," the authors chronicle the story in detail, beginning with the hiring of Carly Fiorina, who was CEO between 1999 and 2005. After Fiorina's departure, the company cycled through four CEOs until 2011, including the current CEO Meg Whitman. Mark Hurd served as the HP leader between 2005 and 2010. Hurd's successor, Leo Apotheker, served only one year, from 2010 to 2011. Whitman, who had been serving as an independent member of the board before her tenure began in 2011, appears to be a good choice for the company, and in the last four years, she has brought the company much needed stability and a new strategic focus for the future.[9]

The Real HP Story

Still, beyond the disruption that this chaotic CEO turnover caused, the real story at HP was the consequence of a dysfunctional board making one bad CEO choice after another. CEO selection is difficult enough when a board is in full harmony and is constructively focused on effective succession; it's impossible when disarray prevails. So, what happened at this highly successful, global technology giant to prompt its board to make such highly destructive decisions?

A string of disappointing earnings reports ended Carly Fiorina's tenure. Mark Hurd was party to an embarrassing scandal that divided the board and prompted his dismissal after a six-to-four split vote. Leo Apotheker had a change of heart about selling HP's struggling PC division, and it was that flip-flop that resulted in a 20 percent drop in stock value; the board soon after showed Apotheker the door.

Larcker and Tayan's 2011 article drew the following very relevant conclusions about board governance:

- Two primary responsibilities of a board are the approval of corporate strategy and the selection of the CEO to refine and execute that strategy.
- The hallmark of a well-governed company is a reliable system for the development of internal managerial talent.[10]

Clearly, these governance priorities eluded the HP board during the tenures of Fiorina, Hurd, and Apotheker. It should be noted, however, that even if a critical decision is made by a group of highly experienced people, it is still entirely possible to get it dead wrong instead of "right." This reality does not, of course, absolve any board from responsibility for the choices that it makes and the need for effective board governance practices.

As Eric Jackson noted in his 2012 *Forbes* blog criticizing the HP board, "It's difficult enough to find the best CEO when going outside the organization, but if the board does not have its act together it is nearly impossible for a board to be effective."[11]

How to Make the Right Choice

How can boards ensure that they've made the best possible leadership choice throughout a CEO's tenure? As we've noted elsewhere in this book, CEO assessment is not a single event but, rather, a continuous process of evaluation that takes place during every interaction that a board has with a company's CEO. This interaction includes both principle (such as board meetings) and secondary (quarterly earnings calls) opportunities that help board members assess a CEO's performance.

- **Board Meetings:** Board meetings are a perfect opportunity for members to observe how the CEO interacts with other senior team members as they answer questions or lead discussions. Sometimes meetings are held away from the boardroom (perhaps annually or biannually) to conduct in-depth strategy reviews or to visit company facilities. These meetings present another good opportunity for board members to interact with the CEO's team and other key member of management, including possible successors to the CEO.
- **Direct Board and CEO Meetings:** Regularly scheduled sessions with the board and the CEO, without any other members of management being present, offers a good opportunity for open dialogue on any issue, including long-term and short-term succession plans, problems with direct reports, and strategic issues. These meetings and conversations are also an excellent way for the board to gain an understanding of how the CEO approaches and solves challenges. Some boards hold these sessions during dinner or perhaps during breakfast. But, no matter when they are scheduled, such meetings engender a very open and forthright relationship, and such open dialogue should be scheduled during every board meeting. With rare exceptions, this forum is appropriate for discussion of almost any topic.

- **Annual Assessments:** An annual assessment yields very specific information about a CEO's performance. Any observations or recommendations that emerge from this assessment should be communicated to the CEO by at least two board members, including the lead director or a proxy and, depending the board's structure, the chair of the Compensation Committee or the chair of the Governance/Nominating Committee.
- **Executive Sessions of the Board:** An executive session is a meeting for independent directors alone, without the CEO. During these discussions, the role of the lead director is critical to ensure a constructive discussion that addresses the individual or collective concerns of the board. This meeting is critical to the building of confidence within the board that the board has chosen the right CEO.
- **Quarterly Earnings Calls:** A quarterly earnings call represents an excellent opportunity for board members to observe how the CEO and the CEO's team present the results and handle the analyst's questions. Members should pay close attention to those questions, since they offer a window into how the market is viewing the company's challenges and execution. Note that not every CEO is comfortable handling these important calls, so this job is sometimes deferred to the chief financial officer (CFO).

IS A ROBUST SUCCESSION PLAN IN PLACE?

The full board, not a committee, is responsible for agreeing on who the short-term emergency successor should be if something happens to the CEO. A good practice is to develop a formal emergency plan that outlines in detail who should be contacted and in what order if such an unexpected event takes place.

One of the best ways to ensure that a robust succession plan is in place is to establish the practice of conducting an annual review of the company's succession and management development plans.

The board also has the responsibility of ensuring that the right future leaders of the business are being developed. Ideally, this detailed succession plan is an annual presentation to the board that is also part of a robust, active human resource development plan.

Generally, these individuals report directly to the CEO and often are considered a potential successor to the chief executive; other candidates below this reporting level are considered as high-potential candidates for leadership. In addition, the board must be comfortable with the difficult job of discussing performance issues with the CEO.

Regardless of whether the choice of successor is a member of the board or a senior officer not yet considered to be the long-term candidate for CEO successor, it is essential that a board reach a consensus on this critical matter. What the board must avoid is making this decision in an emergency situation. The days are long past when a board accepts that the Chairman/CEO's succession directive is contained in an envelope that is kept in a middle desk drawer.

DETERMINING THE RIGHT STRATEGY

While it's true that the board does not run the organization, board members still expect the CEO and the CEO's management team to present an effective strategic plan and to execute it effectively. Regardless of the procedural matters that occupy the board's time and attention, the most effective boards find ways to devote sufficient time to this critical subject. It is not an unreasonable request to add an extra day to a board's schedule each year to review the strategic plan and to fully reflect on both the soundness of the strategic plan and the risks in its execution. Quite often speakers such as investment bankers or consultants from outside the company are included in these meetings, because they can provide insight on particular issues. Here are some other activities that contribute to determining the right strategy:

- **Regularly Scheduled Meetings:** One of the biggest benefits of the regularly scheduled informal meeting between just the CEO and the board of directors is the opportunity for directors to ask questions or to raise doubts about strategic matters in a more open, informal setting without other members of the management team being present.

- **Communication between Scheduled Meetings:** Boards keep attuned to strategic issues and also determine strategy by means of regular communication with the CEO, such as monthly reports about the company that includes analysts' reports or copies of presentations to the investment community.
- **Materials for Board Meeting:** It's important to include materials in board meetings that provide information that is more than an assessment of stock prices and financial data or information about the company's competitors. Understanding and following what is taking place in the competitive marketplace is an important component of tracking the efficacy of the company's strategy. Sometimes apparent strong performance is a consequence of strong industry fundamentals or perhaps even weak fundamentals. Sometimes the company's performance is not as strong as the numbers suggest, and at other times the weak financials do not present a true picture of underlying strength. Boards must make these determinations and judge if the company's strategy is flawed or perhaps lacking in execution. It is no easy job to wade through these many sources of information in order to address fundamental operational questions.

CHAPTER SUMMARY

A corporate board has two main duties to fulfill:

1. Ensure that the right CEO is in place.
2. Watch over the fiduciary interests of the company, shareholders, investors, and all other stakeholders who are impacted by the decisions made by the board.

In addition, there are three key questions that must always be front and center in the minds of all board members:

1. Is the right CEO running the company?
2. Is the company following the right strategy?
3. Is a robust succession plan in place?

Choosing the wrong CEO can be very costly, as the saga of Home Depot's high-profile CEO clearly illustrates. To avoid this mistake, Chapter 3, "Key Board Leadership Roles," offers some effective ways for board members to monitor the CEO's impact on the company and the CEO's fit with the company's cultural and organizational values. These techniques include simple observations at regular board meetings; conducting one-on-one meetings with the board and CEO without other members of management being present; and observations and interactions during annual assessments, executive board sessions, and quarterly earnings calls.

Boards must also ensure that they have enough information to allow them to determine whether the company is following the right strategy. A number of techniques were offered in this chapter, including adding additional time to a board's schedule to review strategic plans and potential risks to the strategy, one-on-one meetings between the CEO and directors, regular reports from the CEO that include analysts' reports about the company, and copies of the CEO's presentations to the investment community. Boards should also insist that complete board briefing materials be provided so that members can independently assess important strategic and operational questions.

Finally, it is the board's responsibility to ensure that both a long-term and a short-term succession plan is always in place.

WHAT'S NEXT?

Corporate boards and their internal governing policies and procedures are directly influenced by both the societal concerns of the moment and the overall vibrancy of the economic landscape. Since every board is unique, each will respond to the same set of external conditions in a way that suits its individual circumstances and culture. Chapter 3, "Key Board Leadership Roles," explores some of the most significant economic and cultural shifts that have occurred over the last twenty years and examines how they have impacted the way boards operate and, ultimately, the decisions that every board makes.

Chapter 3

KEY BOARD LEADERSHIP ROLES

What's in This Chapter?
- Why Leadership Roles Have Changed
- The Debate about Role Separation
- Nonexecutive Chairman/Lead or Presiding Director
- The Challenge of Board Leadership
- Chapter Summary and What's Next

C orporate boards and their internal governing policies and procedures are directly influenced by the societal concerns of the moment and the overall vibrancy of the business environment and economy. As we noted in Chapter 1, "The Changing World of Board Governance: How We Got Here," each board is unique and responds to challenges in ways that suit its individual circumstances and culture. This chapter explores how some of the most game-changing social and economic challenges faced by boards over the last twenty years have altered both governance policies and practices, and, importantly, how CEOs interact with their boards.

As discussed briefly in Chapter 1, the 1990s was an era of economic expansion. Then Secretary of the Treasury Alan Greenspan even characterized those years as a time of "irrational exuberance" in a 1996 speech given at The American Enterprise Institute for Public Policy Research.[1]

The Dow Jones Industrial Average began the decade at 2,563 and climbed year after year during what became known as the dot.com bubble until it reached 11,501 at the end of the cycle. When the bubble burst, the economic fallout across the board was swift and painful for individual and institutional investors who lost billions of dollars, while thousands of employees were left unemployed when the dust settled.

Perhaps the most recognizable examples of Greenspan's "exuberance" was Ken Lay, CEO of Enron, who was praised by every business publication and media outlet as innovative and a shining example of a "new economy maverick."[2] Clearly, such high-flying, profit-taking executives as Lay were very much idolized and apparently could do no wrong. That opinion changed overnight as Enron (and other poster companies for excess, notably WorldCom and Tyco) were revealed as the chief purveyors of corporate malefeasance.

THE DEMISE OF WORLDCOM

WorldCom Files for Bankruptcy—Largest U.S. Case

WorldCom, plagued by the rapid erosion of its profits and an accounting scandal that created billions in illusory earnings, last night submitted the largest bankruptcy filing in United States history.

The bankruptcy is expected to shake an already wobbling telecommunications industry, but is unlikely to have an immediate impact on customers, including the 20 million users of its MCI long-distance service.

The WorldCom filing listed more than $107 billion in assets, far surpassing those of Enron, which filed for bankruptcy last December. The WorldCom filing had been anticipated since the company disclosed in late June that it had improperly accounted for more than $3.8 billion of expenses.[3]

PUBLIC OUTCRY FOR ACTION

The result of these revelations was a public outcry for action, and overnight the public sentiment changed from an attitude that business "could do no wrong" to one of "business could do nothing right." Congress and federal regulators responded by passing the Sarbanes-Oxley Act (SOX) in July 2002, while at the behest of the Securities and Exchange Commission (SEC), the New York Stock Exchange (NYSE), also in July 2002, implemented new and dramatically changed governance requirements in their Listed Company Manual.

Both actions represented a dramatic change in the world of corporate governance. SOX, as passed by Congress, was focused primarily on protecting investors from fraudulent accounting practices, as exemplified by the egregious practices that had taken place at Enron and WorldCom.

Specifically, the provisions in SOX were aimed at ensuring the integrity of financial statements of publicly traded companies. It made the following changes to the internal accounting controls.

- **Public and Independent Oversight of Company Audits:** As an outcome of the Enron collapse, the Chicago-based public accounting firm Arthur Anderson, LLP was found criminally liable and was forced into bankruptcy. As part of SOX, the Public Company Accounting Oversight Board (PCAOB) was created, as their website describes: "The PCAOB is a nonprofit corporation established by Congress to oversee the audits of public companies in order to protect the interests of investors and further the public interest in the preparation of informative, accurate, and independent audit reports."[4]
- A requirement was included to actively improve auditing and corporate governance practices by further defining the independence of the audit committee, requiring the designation of a committee "financial expert" and the committee and board determination of the audit committee members as financially qualified. Further, the committee was given the sole responsibility for hiring the public accounting firm, including the requirement that the firm report directly to the audit committee.

- More accountability and transparency focused on investor protection, including, among other things, the written certification by the chief executive officer (CEO) and chief financial officer (CFO) of the integrity of the quarterly and annual financial reports and statements.
- More independence for auditors and the services that they provide, along with a requirement to rotate audit partners every five years.

Obviously, these were enormous changes for the audit committee and the board. These important changes, with modifications and improvements along the way, as implemented by the PCAOB, continue to this day.

CHANGES IN NYSE LISTING REQUIREMENTS

As noted, coincidental to the passage of the Sarbanes-Oxley Act, the implantation of the new NYSE governance requirements brought far-reaching changes to board governance practices. In fact, as significant as SOX was to the audit committee and management, the new NYSE governance guidelines dramatically altered the governance landscape for directors, the board, and the investor community. The revised Section 303A of the NYSE Listed Company Manual included the following game-changing clauses:

- The board of directors of a publicly listed and traded company must be composed of a majority of independent directors.
- The determination of independence of a director must be affirmed by the board, including no material relationship with the listed company, either directly or as a partner, shareholder, or officer of an organization that has a relationship with the company, including such current employees as the CEO or CFO.
- Listed companies must have a nominating/governance committee, audit committee, and compensation committee composed entirely of independent directors. Other committees are permitted, but these three are required. In the early days following the passage of the regulations, many CEOs had a difficult time

understanding that they could no longer vote as a member of these standing committees.

- An annual performance evaluation of each of the three required standing committees must be conducted.
- The board should conduct a self-evaluation at least annually to determine whether it and its committee are functioning effectively.
- Corporate governance guidelines must address director orientation and continuing education, along with policies limiting the number of boards on which a director may sit and director tenure, retirement, and succession. Finally, the guidelines must outline investor access to management and, as necessary and appropriate, the right to obtain independent advisors.

As significant as these changes were, one section (303A.03 Executive Session) changed the very nature of the relationship between CEOs and their board directors. As stated in the NYSE Listed Company Manual,

To empower non-management directors to serve as a more effective check on management, the nonmanagement director of each listed company must meet at regularly scheduled executive sessions without management.

THE DEBATE OVER THE SEPARATION OF ROLES

Prior to the events of 2001, the question of separation of the roles of chairman and CEO was not at issue. Since that time the issue of whether or not to allow a dual role of Chairman/CEO has become a very contentious one.

For many shareholder groups, particularly the ones that are more activist, there is no question that the two roles should be separate. These activist groups cite the European model, in which a traditionally very strong executive chairman is also a member of management, along with the CEO. Great significance is placed not only on the CEO but also on the executive chairman. Usually, extensive press coverage is focused on both positons.

This arrangement is not always successful, as the recent upheaval at Volkswagen demonstrates. Chairman Fernando Piech, a member of Volkswagen's founding family, endeavored to marshal shareholder support for the removal of the CEO.

The news service Reuters reported on the power struggle on April 15, 2015, under the headline "VW struggles in 'Diplomacy Phase' as Investors Weigh CEO Change." Eventually, Chairman Piech lost his bid to get the support of another family member and significant shareholder, Wolfgang Porsche, and Piech subsequently resigned.[5]

An example in the United States is the debate over whether Robert Iger, currently CEO of Disney, should assume the title of chairman. To put the issue in context, his predecessor, Michael Eisner, was stripped of the title over several very contentious issues with shareholders. When Eisner was finally forced to leave office and Iger became Disney's CEO, the job title did not include that of chairman. However, after a number of years of very strong performance, the board decided to give Iger the dual title of Chairman/CEO.

The Connecticut Retirement Plan and Trust Fund (CRPTF) objected to Iger's receiving the title of chairman in a proxy proposal: "We believe that the role of the Chief Executive Officer and management is to run the business of the company and the role of the board is to oversee management. We believe given these different roles and responsibilities, leadership of the board should be separate from leadership of management."[6]

Large Financial Institution Example

After J.P. Morgan experienced significant losses in their U.K. operations—known as the "London Whale" episode, when a single employee lost billions of dollars on risky trades—activist shareholder groups placed a proxy demand for the separation of the chairmanship from CEO for Jamie Dimon. After a lengthy period of public debate, the company prevailed and Jamie Dimon retained his title as Chairman/CEO; as part of the debate, J.P. Morgan did institute the position of a strengthened lead director.

According to Spencer Stuart's 2014 Board Index report, 53 percent of the S&P 500 companies currently combine the titles of chairman and CEO versus 74 percent in 2004.[7] Some of that change in separation of roles is due to the continuation of historical practices, while others are part of a CEO succession practice. In those cases the current Chairman/CEO gives up the title of CEO, retaining the title of executive chairman in order to facilitate an effective transition in responsibilities. When the executive chairman retires, the CEO normally assumes the title of chairman.

Should CEO and Director Be Separate Roles?

Is it better to separate the role of chairman from that of CEO? Does the separation really enhance board governance and effectiveness?

The answer to these questions may lie in a lack of understanding of how boards function. Do some Chairman/CEOs or CEOs try to control and manage their boards and refuse to share important information? The short answer is "yes," but they are the rare exception. However, whether the CEO is chairman of the board or not, today boards are much more involved and engaged in the board's agenda, committee functions, and operations, and in assuring that the board's responsibilities and fiduciary duties are satisfactorily fulfilled. As noted earlier, the world of board governance changed when the independent directors were required by the new NYSE Listed Company Manual rules to meet alone periodically, without the CEO being present. This requirement allows the independent director to address any and all concerns that he or she may have about the CEO and the CEO's team and strategy, or any other critical issue, including succession planning.

As noted by David F. Larcker and Brian Tayan in the March 14, 2013 *Stanford Closer Look Series* article, "Where Experts Get It Wrong: Independence vs. Leadership in Corporate Governance": "Independence, as beneficial as it may sound, may have less value than we all assume. Many observed structured features of corporate governance have little or no relation to governance qualities. For example, there is little systematic evidence that it benefits a company to have an independent chairman."[8]

Along with arguments on both sides, the largest manager of securities is now weighing in. BlackRock, the largest of such companies, has provided the following statement in their "Proxy Voting Guidelines for U.S. Securities," dated February 2015.

> *We believe that independent leadership is important in the board room. In the U.S. there are two commonly accepted structures for independent board leadership: 1) an independent chairman; and 2) a lead independent director. We assess the experience and governance track record of the independent chairman or lead director to understand capability and suitability to effectively and constructively lead a board. Our expectations of an individual in this role include, but are not limited to: being available to serve as an advisor to the CEO, contributing to the oversight of CEO and management succession planning, and being available to meet with shareholders when they have highly sensitive concerns about management or corporate governance issues. We generally consider the designation of a lead independent director as an acceptable alternative to an independent chair, has a term of at least one year and has powers to: 1) provide formal input into board agendas; 2) call meetings of the independent directors; and 3) preside at meetings of the independent directors. Where a company does not have a lead independent director that meets these criteria, we generally support the separation of chairman and CEO.[9]*

NONEXECUTIVE CHAIRMAN, LEAD DIRECTOR, OR PRESIDING DIRECTOR

The board leadership positions of nonexecutive chairman, lead director, or presiding director have become very important since 2002. A vast majority (90 percent) of S&P 500 companies have either a lead director or a presiding director, while a smaller percentage (28 percent) have an independent chairman.[10] Nevertheless, the switch from familiar meeting protocols that were in place before 2002 has meant re-evaluating fundamental governance practices, including the frequency of the meetings held without the CEO being present, leadership of the discussions during these sessions (the general practice today is that the lead director is in charge of these discussions), and how to best communicate the results of these independent meetings to the larger board.

Defining the Role of Nonexecutive Chairman

The nonexecutive chairman is responsible for calling the board meeting to order and, as appropriate, taking charge of moving the proceedings along. Once the meeting is officially open, normally the nonexecutive chairman turns the meeting over to the CEO, who directs any activities necessary to complete the board's agenda.

During an annual meeting, the nonexecutive chairman usually calls the meeting to order by reading a prepared script in order to ensure that any proxy protocol is followed. The CEO leads the business discussions and answers any relevant questions, unless other members of the board are asked to provide input. This is a brief overview, but perhaps a bit of personal experience might add some value.

About fifteen years ago, I served as the nonexecutive chairman of Nucor, the largest steel producer in the United States, based in Charlotte, North Carolina. At the time the board had just voted to elect Dan DiMicco as its next CEO, so the directors decided that my experience as both a board member and a former CEO would help Dan settle into his new role. As a result I remained the nonexecutive chairman until 2006, when the board decided to acknowledge Dan's well-recognized success by electing him as both chairman and CEO (Dan's record included a significant increase in the stock price). When Dan took over as chairman, I had no duties beyond the nonexecutive chair responsibilities that I noted earlier.

So, what do these three board leadership roles—nonexecutive chairman, lead director, and presiding director—have in common? In the simplest of terms, they act as the honest broker between the CEO and the board, and vice versa. When the executive sessions occur, the lead director has the responsibility of meeting with the CEO to provide direct feedback from the board. These one-on-one feedback sessions usually occur immediately after the independent board meetings. However, it is sometimes constructive to ask the CEO to join the session at the end of discussion so that the CEO can clearly understand the sentiment and suggestions of the independent board.

THE CHALLENGE OF BOARD LEADERSHIP

Leading an effective executive session is an art that allows all points of view and concerns to be heard without allowing the session to become unnecessarily protracted and unproductive. Knowing when to allow further deliberation or when to move on takes skill.

A good practice—and really a necessary one—is for the lead director to meet in person, or communicate with, the CEO between meetings. The purpose might be to discuss the agenda or the schedule for the next meeting, or the discussion might revolve around how to engage the board between meetings on a pending acquisition, merger, divestiture, or other key strategic move. How often, where, and how these meetings should take place is determined by the physical location of the CEO and the lead director. Sometimes it is convenient to schedule a face-to-face meeting, whereas at other times connecting by phone between meetings makes more sense.

Challenges of Transition and Letting Go

The lead director plays a critical role before, during, and after a CEO transition. For example, a lead director helps ensure that the timing of the transition is right and that questions about board membership status are answered. In many ways the lead director often acts as the honest broker between the incumbent CEO and the board by ensuring that all voices are heard, that mutual concerns are addressed, and that an effective transition is facilitated.

Letting Go of Leadership
Being an "honest broker" is especially important if the incumbent Chairman/CEO or CEO is having difficulty letting go of his or her

leadership position. Certainly, the board should be engaged in the process of CEO transition, but the lead director plays the most critical role in assuring a successful and smooth transition. The lead director also plays a key role if the board decides that the current Chairman/CEO should step down and assume a position of executive chairman in order to allow new leadership to transition in. A recent example of this strategy occurred recently when Cisco's long-time chairman, John Chambers, announced that he would step down as CEO and take a position as executive chairman. As reported in the May 4, 2015 edition of the *New York Times*, Chambers stepped down to allow a younger, new generation of leadership to succeed him.[11]

In these circumstances the lead director plays a critical role, interacting with both the incumbent and the board in order to ensure a successful transition and to determine the duties and responsibilities of the executive chairman, including how the former CEO will spend his or her time during the transition and when the CEO will officially leave the board.

Communicating with Shareholders

Lead directors are also playing an increasingly important role in communicating with shareholders on behalf of the board and the company. Sometimes the lead director is accompanied by the CEO, and at other times, with fellow directors or sometimes alone. Until recently, such direct communication has been an exception. You can easily find governance guidelines concerning such communication on the websites of many companies. Here is an example from Lowe's "Governance Guidelines":

Board Interaction with Institutional Investors, Media, and Customers

"The board believes that the management and specifically the Chief Executive Officer or his designee, speak for Lowe's and in Nucor Corporation governance guidelines."[12]

And here's an example from Nucor's "Governance Principles":

Communication with Third Parties

"Management and, specifically, the CEO and his or her designee, speak for Nucor Corporation. It is expected that directors would not speak for the company except in unusual circumstances."[13]

Institutional Investor Activity

In my role as lead director for one company, I met with shareholders both alone and with fellow directors and the company CEO. Since the meetings took place prior to a potential proxy fight, I also met with Institutional Shareholder Services (ISS) to explain my company's side of the argument. Large institutional shareholders such as BlackRock, Vanguard, and others now take a public stance on certain governance matters or regarding a specific position on a company's proxy vote.

The CEO of Vanguard, William NcNabb, went to great lengths in a February 2015 letter to large corporations to explain why an ongoing dialogue between the company and Vanguard was not only invited but also expected: "The relationship between the corporate boards and large shareholders is important, but too often, there is precious little communication between the two parties. The case for effective engagement is compelling for both shareholders and boards."[14]

Larry Fink, chairman and CEO of BlackRock, echoed this sentiment in a letter to corporations dated March 3, 2015: "Asset managers like BlackRock also have an important role to play, which is why we engage actively with companies on the key governance factors that in our experience support long-term, sustainable, financial performance."[15]

In the future expect more calls for communication between the board and major shareholders, and an increasing responsibility for the lead director to be an "honest broker."

CHAPTER SUMMARY

In this chapter we explored how some of the most game-changing social and economic events of the last twenty years have reshaped governance policy and practices as well as the relationship between CEOs and their boards.

Specifically, the demise of Enron, WorldCom, and Tyco in 2002 were offered as the capstone event to a long period of corporate excess that began in the 1990s. The corporate malfeasance that was exposed when these companies filed for bankruptcy prompted a series of legislative and regulatory actions in 2002 that included passage of the Sarbanes-Oxley Act, significant changes to the NYSE Listed Company Manual, and new SEC regulatory requirements.

This chapter used these major upheavals in the marketplace and the impact on corporate board governance as the background for a thorough discussion of board leadership roles—specifically, the efficacy of allowing a CEO to also serve as board chairman.

In addition, this chapter provided a substantial discussion of the nonexecutive chairman's role (also called the lead director or presiding director). Most companies have either a lead director or a presiding director, whereas about one-third have an independent chairman.

Finally, the chapter offers a set of useful guidelines for effective board leadership, along with useful tips on effectively communicating with shareholders.

WHAT'S NEXT?

As the world of board governance continues to change, activist groups of shareholders approach companies with various proposals, ongoing requests are made for a split of the Chairman/CEO roles, proxy access is either in place or about to be voted on in the next proxy, and there is continuing pressure to have a satisfactory advisory vote on pay, the importance of the role of lead director will continue if not increase. As contentious and important issues are brought before the board and shareholders for votes, the need for the lead director to facilitate open and constructive dialogue between independent directors and the CEO of the company will be more important than ever.

As for the debate over the separation of roles, it will continue to be found on the front pages of the business press. Every time an activist shareholder group feels as if the company is not performing and/or accuses the company of possible wrongdoing, the proxy for the next annual meeting is likely to include a request for the separation of the roles of chairman and CEO. The response is also likely to be that separation of the roles is not necessary as the board embraces the role of the "strong lead director," including the right to call a meeting of the board, direct involvement in the setting of the agenda of the board meetings, and so forth.

Chapter 4

BOARD CULTURE

What's in This Chapter?
- Understanding Board Culture
- The Three Elements of Board Culture
- The Leadership and Board Performance Cycle
- Transforming Board Culture
- Chapter Summary and What's Next

C orporate boards, like any other gathered group of business or community leaders, are organized with two key outcomes in mind: to make good decisions and to identify emerging opportunities that will add value to their organization. Unfortunately, this seemingly crystal clear mission and the logical results that one might expect to emerge from such gatherings are often muddled by a whole range of group dynamics and human factors that seriously impact effectiveness and performance. This chapter examines why these human factors frequently derail the efforts of even the best corporate boards and provides research-based techniques that ensure mistakes that stand in the way of corporate boards attempting to accomplish their vital governance role are avoided.

UNDERSTANDING BOARD CULTURE

The term *culture* was first used by researcher Elliott Jaques in 1951 to describe the unique climate or personality of an organization, or, as Jaques characterized it at the time, "the way things get done around here."[1] We define *board culture* a little more precisely. For us, board culture is *the unique, shared mind-set of a group of directors that dictates norms of engagement, communication, conflict management, and problem-solving processes.*

Researchers such as Edgar H. Schein have refined this description of organizational culture. His 1985 seminal work on this topic identified four distinct seen and unseen layers of culture that Schein labeled as

1. Patterns of Behavior
2. Norms
3. Values
4. Basic Assumptions[2]

Patterns of Behavior: The patterns of communication, decision making, and conflict management practices are often referred to as "the way we do things around here." This observable aspect of board culture also dictates dress code and the degree of formality.

Norms: Just below the surface of visibility are norms, which are the "unwritten rules" of engagement and represent what is expected, rewarded, and punished within the board.

Values: Values exist at a deeper level and reflect the underlying beliefs and values of the organization as a whole. While norms directly dictate acceptable and unacceptable behaviors, values are more deeply embedded and only indirectly influence behaviors.

Basic Assumptions: At the deepest level of culture are the basic assumptions of the board, which represent the tacit, "as-if" assumptions of the group and are often unspoken; in many instances, the board is not consciously aware of them. Primal issues such as abundance, scarcity, safety, and fear are grounded in this deepest level of culture.

A BRIEF REVIEW OF BOARD CULTURE RESEARCH

A pivotal and defining moment in board research occurred in the late 1990s when Daniel F. Forbes and Francis J. Milliken found that "intervening processes," or *group dynamics*, create unique cultures that impact board discussion and dialogue, and, ultimately, variances in corporate performance.[3]

Prior to this seminal work, research on board governance focused on structure, rules, procedures, and committee responsibilities. Ongoing research has consistently demonstrated the importance of board culture and interpersonal dynamics on board decision making, problem solving, and overall performance.

Jeffrey A. Sonnenfeld argued in 2002 that what separates exemplary boards from average or below-average boards is *social* and not structural, stating that boards are living social systems and that high-performing boards are grounded in the "virtuous cycle" of respect, trust, and candor.[4] Researchers Kathleen Eisenhardt, Jean Kahwajy, and L. J. Bourgeois in 1997 found that this shared respect and trust among board members allows even the most "sacred cow" discussions to occur without impacting the high-performing companies studied.[5]

More recently the *Director Notes* publication from The Conference Board (2014) suggests that the overall team dynamics created by the board culture is more important than the qualifications, skills, and experiences of individual directors.[6] In fact, this report suggests that board assessment should include a measure of the overall culture of the board as a whole, in addition to individual director peer-to-peer assessments.

EXAMPLES ILLUSTRATING SCHEIN'S MODEL OF CULTURE AND BOARD DYNAMICS

Since research-based conclusions are often best understood (despite their precision) by example, following are a few examples that explain how Schein's conclusions about cultural formation might be manifested in the real world.

A Nominally Engaged Board

Imagine a board whose members are only nominally engaged. Dissent and conflict are the norm within the group. Multiple agendas frequently circulate simultaneously, causing confusion. Open disagreements occur frequently among the board members, the CEO, and the senior management team. Moreover, the prevailing assumption among the board members is that the CEO and the senior management team have a hidden agenda, so nothing that leadership says is taken at face value.

How would you characterize this board's culture by applying Schein's four levels? Here is how we would analyze this board's culture:

Patterns of Behavior: Disagreement, dissent, open conflict, and tardiness.

Norms: Members are distracted and often challenge the CEO and the senior management team.

Values: A "trust but verify" atmosphere underlies board interactions.

Basic Assumptions: People cannot be trusted, and we live in a "zero-sum" world of scarcity.

A Highly Engaged Board

Now, imagine a board that is characterized by highly engaged directors. Robust and candid conversations occur often among the board members, the CEO, and the senior management team. The agenda is well understood and is universally shared. Directors are always prepared, and the group deftly balances candor and objectivity, leading to trust. The group is optimistic and excited about the future.

How would you characterize this board's culture by applying Schein's four levels? Given this second scenario, here's how we would characterize this board's culture:

Patterns of Behavior: Engagement, candor, and respect for differing opinions.
Norms: Engagement, punctuality, respectful listening, and questioning.
Values: Trust of the CEO and other directors; open to innovation and change.
Basic Assumptions: People are trustworthy, and we live in a world of generative abundance.

THE THREE ELEMENTS OF BOARD CULTURE

The previous examples illustrate Schein's concepts but beg the question: what creates a "scarcity" mind-set and culture versus one of "abundance?" Schein's work illustrates an important distinction about the multidimensional nature of board culture: one level impacts another, and board culture is founded on basic assumptions. However, just because you understand the basic assumptions driving behaviors, this doesn't mean that this insight will ensure effectiveness, as illustrated later in this chapter when we introduce our model, *The Leadership and Board Performance Cycle* (see Figure 4.2). Before we discuss practical strategies for understanding and managing board culture, it is important to understand where and how board culture is developed and reinforced. Too often we want to blame the "leader" as the culprit behind a dysfunctional board. And, although the style of the CEO has a definite impact on board culture and performance, it is only one of several factors that impact that culture.

As illustrated above, board culture is complex, interrelated, and multifaceted. While there are numerous contextual aspects that are unique to each board, our experience suggests that board culture is created and sustained by three primary factors:

1. Individual personalities of board members.
2. Larger context or "macro-environment" factors impacting the business.
3. CEO leadership style.

Individual Personalities of Board Members

Although the overall group culture and dynamics of the board ultimately determine its effectiveness, individual personalities matter. In fact, they matter a lot. There is an old adage that one director cannot create a high-performing board, but one director can do a lot of damage.

Research using the "Big 5" personality model has been used to measure personality in an effort to predict leadership effectiveness. The "Big 5" personality model consists of five "Super Traits" that determine individual personality and style, as seen in Figure 4.1.

Although there is limited research that correlates the impact of personality with organizational success, there have been some studies conducted. For example, in 1999 Timothy Judge, Chad Higgins, Carl Thoresen, and Murray Barrick found that leaders who score higher in "Conscientiousness," the trait of being organized, focused, and efficient, achieve greater levels of success. They may be extroverted and outspoken, or they may be introverted and more reserved. In either case, directors with this trait are more likely to be prepared for board meetings and to be more focused on performance.[7]

Another trait, "Neuroticism," measures individual differences related to anxiety, anger, and impulsiveness. Leaders with higher scores for this trait are often correlated with being moody, temperamental, and envious. At their best, these directors can also be charming, charismatic, and self-confident, coming across as bold and visionary. Not surprisingly, however, this trait tends to predict lower levels of empathy and collaboration, as Michael Maccoby noted in 2004. Directors with this trait are likely to make favorable first impressions, but they can become frustrated and disruptive.[8]

Another example is the trait of "Agreeableness," which is related to being trusting, modest, empathetic, and collaborative. Leaders who score high in this trait are dependable, effective listeners; are inclusive; and prefer to work together as a team to accomplish goals. With this approach, they are successful at producing long-term results.

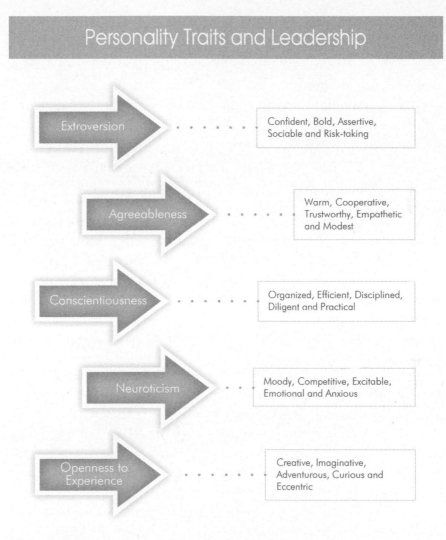

Figure 4.1   Personality Traits and Leadership

The Larger Context or "Macro-Environment" Factors Impacting the Business

The second factor impacting board culture is the larger macro-environment, or context, in which the organization exists. For example, is the business growing and expanding, or is it contracting? Are technology and the global environment helping to drive innovation, or are they making the organization's products and services obsolete? In addition to these macro factors, contemporary issues such as shareholder activism and regulatory oversight impact board culture. For an example of how these issues impact board culture, let's examine shareholder activism.

Activist shareholders are more prevalent today than ever before. Many activist shareholders who take a significant position in a given stock are not necessarily seeking a seat on the board. Rather, they desire to have a direct line to the CEO and management team to express their concerns, provide advice, and influence the activities of the organization. Although this situation is undoubtedly more disruptive for the management team, it can and does impact the dynamics of the board and, as a result, the board culture.

On occasion, activist shareholders will demand a seat on the board, which leads to a much deeper level of engagement, not only with the management team, but also with the board itself. Often, at least at the outset, these shareholder board members are regarded skeptically by the other board members because they have come by their board seat in a coercive fashion. They often have goals that may be short term in nature and perhaps inconsistent with the longer-term vision held by the board. In the worst case, this type of scenario can be very disruptive to the culture and dynamics of the board by severely damaging open, honest dialogue in the boardroom and creating tension among board members on key strategic issues. In some cases this can lead to more hallway and off-line discussions between board members instead of a healthy debate around the boardroom table.

Longer-Term Strategy

In the best circumstances, however, over time the activist shareholder comes to better understand the organization's longer-term strategy and the existing board comes to understand the activist shareholder's views as well. When it works, these opposing views can be reconciled and the benefit to the organization can be significant. This is exactly what happened when an activist shareholder took a strong position in the Family Dollar stock and negotiated a board seat as a result. Pamela Davies, a Director at Family Dollar, explains:

> *The early skepticism that the board felt for its newest board member cast him largely as an outsider focused only on a short-term profit goal without regard for the longer-term performance of the company. Over time, however, the barriers to understanding one another broke down, and the board began to work collaboratively toward what was arguably a much better outcome for the company.*[9]

In this instance, the board was able to reclaim a more dynamic culture because all of the directors were able to find common ground.

> *When it works well, it is my belief that an activist shareholder with an open mind and a willingness to listen to the existing board's rationale can bring value to the company by sharing his or her views on the company that come through a different lens. Yes, activists can be extremely disruptive, both to the board and the management team. But if managed effectively, they can also contribute greatly to the performance of the company if the board culture is adaptable, and a common vision, along with common ground, can be found.*[10]

CEO Leadership Style

Of the three elements we have noted that impact board culture, the leadership style of the CEO has the most impact on board dynamics and culture. Yes, the board's overall culture ultimately determines the dynamics of the board, as do the individual personalities of board members, the overall health of the business, external economic conditions, and the competitive and regulatory environment faced by the organization. Those factors notwithstanding, the style of the CEO directly impacts the board in a number of ways, including access to senior management and critical information, and a certain degree of process management during the actual board meetings. Again, as the old adage reminds us, one person cannot create success alone, but one person can do a lot of damage.

Research into CEO leadership style and its impact on board performance is limited. Research in this area won't allow us to draw any consistent conclusions for the creation of a single set of board governance "best practices" related to style because of so many complex, competing factors that impact business performance. However, there are some findings that are relevant for this discussion, and they deserve some degree of caution in interpretation. For example, the personality characteristic of "Narcissism," which is the trait of being selfish, proud, and vain, should have negative outcomes, right? Well, not necessarily.

Narcissistic Leaders

Sometimes even the most narcissistic leaders create positive results, while in other cases these traits produce negative, ineffective organizational outcomes. That's because situational context is everything. Researchers have noted that there are two kinds of narcissists: productive and unproductive. Productive narcissists are visionary, bold, charming, charismatic, and courageous. In the right positive environment, these characteristics support the success of a leader and his or her company. However, in a difficult or challenging business environment, these same characteristics lead to failure, because a lack of self-awareness leads to unrealistic goals, delusions of grandeur, and paranoia. For example, former Health-South Corp. CEO Richard Scrushy has been cited by Sue Shellenbarger as an example of a manipulative personality, a "classic, good salesman."[11] He is charismatic and charming but also very difficult on those who confront or disagree with him. He was fired by the board in 2003 after regulators uncovered a multibillion dollar accounting error, and he ended up serving prison time for fraud and bribery.

Example of Context

Here's another example that demonstrates how context trumps any preconceived notions about the positive or negative impact of a particular leadership style. A controlling, autocratic leadership style might be more effective during a time of crisis or to lead a corporate turnaround strategy, despite the many downsides to this leadership style. Boards charged with finding a leader to steer their company through difficult times should always gauge leadership style in the context of the challenge faced. This same principle also applies to the process of identifying board leaders.

Stanford researchers David F. Larcker and Brian Tayan point to the critical role of context in their 2013 article, "Where Experts Get It Wrong: Independence vs. Leadership in Corporate Governance." The article cites the publicly reported disagreements aired in 2004 when the Disney Corporation's board stripped then-CEO Michael Eisner of his chairmanship. Shareholders objected to Eisner's performance and management style, depicted widely in the media as "brilliant," "domineering," and "combative."[12]

Larcker and Tayan write that current CEO and chairman Robert Iger's personality—described as "modest" and "exhibiting good judgment and grace under fire"—is very different from Eisner's. They argue that "independence" of the CEO and Chairman position for the sake of independence, without consideration of personality and style and the larger macro-environment, misses the most important elements of leadership effectiveness and, ultimately, corporate performance. This example illustrates both the impact of personality and leadership style on effectiveness, and perhaps more importantly, on the culture and performance of the board.[13]

A Lead Director Network (2010) update suggested that irrespective of individual personalities, environmental challenges, and CEO style, there are five defining director characteristics that determine board performance, and they follow.[14]

FIVE CHARACTERISTICS OF HIGH-PERFORMING BOARDS

Many factors impact board performance, including five characteristics of high-performing lead directors:

1. Understand the business.
2. Have the right expertise, background, and unique insight to fulfill their role.
3. Are willing to invest the necessary time and energy on the board and the company.
4. Have a strong working relationship with the CEO.
5. Ensure that the board's culture is "dynamic" and blends collegiality with candor.

THE LEADERSHIP AND BOARD PERFORMANCE CYCLE

Appreciating board culture and group dynamics requires understanding what creates and sustains the board's unique personality or culture. Board culture is created and sustained primarily by three discrete components: the personalities of the individual directors, the broader context or macro-environment in which the company operates, and the style of the lead director. Although there is ongoing debate about which element impacts board culture the most, research indicates that the leader's style is the most important.[15]

Impact of Style

It is vital to highlight the impact of a leader's style on board culture. To really understand board leadership and to create a "dynamic" culture with higher levels of director engagement, collegial candor, and pathways to effective decision making requires a much more nuanced examination: first, of the four lead roles—chair, nonexecutive chair, lead director, and presiding director—and,

BOARD AND GROUP DEFINITION

We use "board" and "group" interchangeably in this chapter and define them as three or more people who share a common goal, since physical proximity is not necessary to meet this definition of a group or a board. Likewise, directors may spend very little time physically together, but because they share a common goal, language, and affiliation, they meet the definition of a group and are subject to the principles of small-group behavior.

second, of the four distinct leadership styles based on the dominant motive or need of the leader:

- *Achiever* (Achievement Need)
- *Affirmer* (Affiliation Need)
- *Asserter* (Power Need)
- *Actualized* (Self-Actualization Need)

From a board governance perspective, it is critical to note that each of the four leadership styles creates and fosters a unique board culture. Three of the four leadership styles—*Achiever*, *Affirmer*, and *Asserter*—create a less than optimal board culture and directly impact communication, problem solving, decision making, and, ultimately, director engagement.

The Detached Culture—Achiever Leadership Style

The sad irony in life is that individuals who have a very high need for achievement, *Achievers*, create the lowest performing culture—*Detached*. Because of their need for absolute perfection, *Achievers* sweat every detail while micromanaging their teams. This dynamic plays out in the boardroom as well. *Achievers* are often too bogged down in the details and attempt not only to manage but also often to micromanage the business.

As a result, this culture is grounded in emotions of anger and apathy, and the resulting impact on the board from a group dynamics perspective is detachment. Directors express anger either aggressively, with open conflict and personal attacks, or passively, by disengaging psychologically or physically. Psychological disengagement manifests when directors become more interested in their mobile phones, iPads, or laptops than in the board meeting. Physical disengagement occurs when directors habitually arrive late, leave early, or miss meetings altogether. Whether the anger is expressed actively or passively, directors in a *Detached* culture are not in the optimal position for engaging in candid discussions, healthy debate, and rational decision making. The most likely group decision-making pitfall facing this board culture is *Groupthink*, which will be discussed in the next chapter.

The Dramatic Culture—Affirmer Leadership Style

Now, imagine the extreme opposite end of the spectrum from a *Detached* culture and replace anger with kindness, rudeness with politeness, and despair with hope. At first this kind of board culture might sound more appealing, but it often results in the same degree of poor decision making and director disengagement. The *Dramatic* culture is created and sustained by leaders who are primarily motivated out of the need for affiliation, who are *Affirmers*, and who focus on maintaining warm, harmonious, interpersonal relationships. These leaders want and need to be accepted and approved by the board at all costs. To this end, the board norm is one of politeness and friendliness to the extreme. Difficult or uncomfortable discussions are avoided or tabled for "off-line" conversations that rarely occur. Although it is warm and personally supportive, the *Dramatic* culture lacks collegial candor and frankness. Members often self-censor to avoid breaking the group norm of politeness and agreement.

This culture is grounded in the emotion of frustration. Directors are friendly and polite on the surface, but this norm of "niceness" supersedes the need for healthy debate and conflict. Because candor and conflict are often avoided, directors often leave meetings feeling frustrated and exasperated with the lack of progress or action. The most common group decision-making pitfall with the *Dramatic* culture is *The Abilene Paradox*, which will be discussed in the next chapter.

The Dependent Culture—Asserter Leadership Style

It stands to reason that the majority of business leaders have a high need for power and thus exhibit the *Asserter* leadership style. The resulting culture developed and sustained by this style is *Dependent*. This is the most common culture in Corporate America, whether in Fortune 500 companies or nonprofit organizations. The *Dependent* culture is grounded in fear and anxiety, with its chief attribute being *caution*.

As previously discussed, the *Asserter* style is results oriented and effective in the short term, especially during a crisis. However, this style and the fear that it engenders is not sustainable, and the long-term impact is quite dysfunctional. In a *Dependent* culture, directors look to their powerful leader for assurance, relying too heavily on his or her previous "track record" of accomplishments. Under stress, this leadership style can be dominating and autocratic, often shutting down attempts at open communication when it is needed most.

Managing Up

Although *Asserters* are often extremely candid and blunt, they do not appreciate or tolerate any dissension. Members hesitate to speak out or to challenge the leader, which often leads to poor decision making. This culture is often difficult to identify because *Asserters* are very adept at "managing up," meaning that they create and maintain favorable impressions with their boss, but often at the expense of their team and direct reports. Thus, while the organization may suffer, they often enjoy a favorable impression from the board. It is critical for directors to engage other members of the senior management team to assess the impact of the leader's style on the organization as a whole. The norm of this culture is to "follow the leader," and as a result, the board decision making for a *Dependent* culture often leads to either *Groupthink* or *The Abilene Paradox*.

The Dynamic Culture—Actualized Leadership Style

Leaders who are driven primarily by the need for Self-Actualization often exhibit seemingly contradictory elements in their style. For example, they may be charismatic in a public setting, but often they long for solitude. *Actualized* leaders care deeply for their teammates and their organizations, but that does not inhibit them from making difficult decisions or providing real-time feedback.

Unlike the *Affirmers*, who default to politeness, *Actualized* leaders default to candor. Unlike *Achievers*, who prefer routine and predictability, *Actualized* leaders are spontaneous and enjoy novelty. And, unlike *Asserters*, who crave control and have trouble trusting others, *Actualized* leaders humbly share their power and ask for input, while implicitly trusting others to make decisions and take appropriate actions. While *Actualized* leaders have a high need for achievement, care about their teammates, and are candid and decisive, they exhibit unique characteristics that create and sustain a *Dynamic* board culture.

For example, they understand the business but are not at all interested in getting bogged down in irrelevant details or trying to micromanage the board. They are strategic and conceptual, and they accept ambiguity and uncertainty as part of life. *Actualized* leaders tend to be more realistic and quick to "confront the brutal facts," while trusting others and always being willing to ask for help, input, and guidance. Although they share many of the characteristics of *Asserters*, they use their power for the best interests of the organization as opposed to personal ego gratification. These leaders share focus on the strategic and unknown, but they do not feel compelled to be in control or to always be "right." Finally, and perhaps most importantly, *Actualized* leaders see the world from a sense of abundance as opposed to scarcity, and their motivation has profound impacts on culture.

The Leadership Cycle

Clearly, the *Actualized* leadership style creates the highest performing *dynamic* board culture that is characterized by open, candid communication and high levels of engagement and board and

THE BOARD PERFORMANCE CYCLE

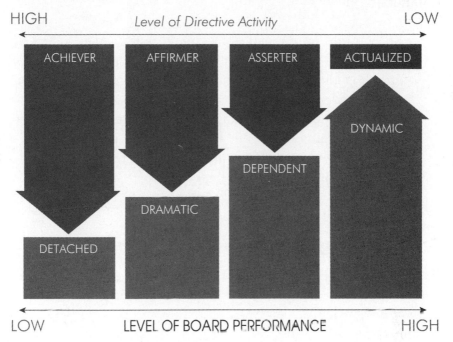

Figure 4.2 The Board Performance Cycle

organizational commitment.[16] Actualized leaders welcome diverse opinions and are adept at questioning their own assumptions about the internal organization and the broader, external environment. The leader and board members treat each other in a respectful, collegial manner and have meetings that are more efficient, since candor allows for honest discussions and debate. All of these qualities allow the board to focus on its primary role of guiding the business toward success.

The leadership cycle shown in Figure 4.2 illustrates the impact of the leader's style and the resulting degree of his or her directive activity on board culture and performance.

TRANSFORMING BOARD CULTURE

Transforming individual attitudes and preconceptions in ways that impact behavior is not easy; the path to change for a board leader is no different than anywhere else and requires the same three conditions:

1. Recognition on the part of the board that change is needed.
2. Recognition on the part of the leader (e.g., lead director, presiding director, nonexecutive chair, CEO, etc.) that his or her leadership style is creating and reinforcing a less than optimal culture, and an expression by the leader of a sincere desire to change.
3. An honest and candid assessment of the "current state" and a commitment, on the part of the board, to create an action plan for making the necessary changes in order to achieve the desired results—a more *Dynamic* culture.

Transforming the *Detached* Group Culture

The *Detached* culture is the least effective level of group development and culture. It often leads to poor decisions as a result of *Groupthink*. Below are suggested practices and steps to help transform a *Detached* culture:

- Provide candid feedback to the lead director and/or CEO, letting him or her know the impact of his or her style on the board's culture.
- Allow the lead director to acknowledge and vent his or her anger and frustration, often best accomplished with a formal board assessment.
- Resolve issues of power, authority, and responsibility among the lead director, the CEO, the board as a whole, and committees.
- Develop and implement board decision-making processes that facilitate director engagement, candid input, and frank discussions.
- Ensure that all directors participate in and adopt a "no cell phones" policy to ensure that all members are participating equally.

Transforming the *Dramatic* Group Culture

The *Dramatic* culture represents a lower level of group development, in which members are committed to each other but often at the expense of the group's performance. This culture is marked by excessive idealism, conflict avoidance, and unrealistic expectations for the future. The decision-making pitfall most common in this instance is *The Abilene Paradox*, and the following strategies can be implemented to transform the *Dramatic* culture:

- Consider showing *The Abilene Paradox* video or providing the article about it so that board members understand and relate to the concept of "mismanaged agreement."
- Encourage directors to provide honest and critical feedback to the lead director, the CEO, or the board as a whole.
- Confront the group about poor performance, unrealistic expectations, or obvious problems.
- Set challenging or even audacious performance goals for the organization and group standards for the board.
- Appoint individual members to serve as "devil's advocate" to critique the group's performance, plans, and decisions.

Transforming the *Dependent* Group Culture

The *Dependent* culture represents the most common group culture, in which members soften their true opinions or practice outright self-censorship. This culture is marked by excessive reliance on the board's leader, and the following strategies can be implemented to transform the *Dependent* culture:

- Involve all board members in developing specific goals and assessing performance of the lead director, the board, and the organization.
- Set and adhere to a schedule that facilitates director interaction with all members of the senior executive team, and encourage senior executives to make presentations to the board.
- Allow members to clarify and communicate their roles and expectations to the entire group, including any frustrations that they may be experiencing.
- Encourage the lead director and/or the CEO to delegate more effectively.

Maintaining the *Dynamic* Group Culture

The *Dynamic* culture represents the highest level of group development and board performance. Members are rational and responsible, and they communicate directly and honestly with each other. There is a high level of engagement with the board and the overall organization, and directors are committed to each other. The following strategies are suggested to maintain and optimize a *Dynamic* culture:

- Focus on healthy debate and discussion, and encourage candid feedback.
- Protect the board from too many external distractions or influences.
- Celebrate organizational successes and achievements.
- Provide the necessary resources for the board to perform at optimal levels.

Understanding board culture and group dynamics and applying these suggested strategies will help ensure that your board is candid, respectful, and engaged. As cited earlier, Jeffrey A. Sonnenfeld found that the conventional wisdom that focused only on structure and procedure was less impactful than efforts based on the realization that boards are "social systems." As such, just as much attention should be paid to building trust and encouraging candor as to schedules, procedures, and process.[17]

CHAPTER SUMMARY

Group culture is the essential determinant of effective board communication, problem solving, and decision making. As we have outlined, boards that develop and maintain *Detached*, *Dramatic*, or *Dependent* cultures are much more likely to suffer from dysfunctional patterns of communication and, as such, engage in ineffective problem solving and group decision making. Understanding the impact that the "leader" has on board culture, whether the leader is a CEO or lead director, is crucial for assessing and improving director engagement and board performance.

WHAT'S NEXT?

Chapter 5, "Group Dynamics and Board Decision Making," will explore board decision making and the two classic group decision-making pitfalls: *Groupthink* and *The Abilene Paradox.* We will offer a framework for predicting which dysfunctional group decision-making dynamics your board is most likely to experience, based on your board's culture, and proven strategies for effectively bypassing these common, and often costly, mistakes.

Chapter 5

GROUP DYNAMICS AND BOARD DECISION MAKING

What's in This Chapter?
- Why Working in Groups Is Difficult
- *Groupthink:* Managing Conflict in the Boardroom
- *The Abilene Paradox:* Managing Agreement in the Boardroom
- Optimizing Board Decision Making
- Chapter Summary and What's Next

As we noted earlier in this book, board decision-making practices should be focused on the most important aspects of corporate governance: *Is the right CEO in place? Is the company pursuing the right strategy? Is the succession plan current and viable?* In addition to these three main questions, boards also make critical decisions related to mergers, acquisitions, divestitures, compensation, and shareholder issues.

Accomplishing this mission, as simple as it appears from the outside, is more challenging than you might imagine, because successful decision making depends on the ability of board members to work together effectively. Since human factors and communication processes are involved, working together cooperatively toward the same goals is more difficult than it might at first appear. As we discussed in the previous chapter, the ultimate goal is to develop and maintain a *Dynamic Culture* that encourages honest, collegial debate and candor among board members, which, in turn, will lead to reasoned, rational decisions. Such an environment naturally improves both individual and group communications, and leads to better decisions, since emotion-driven reactions (perceived or real), peer pressure, or irrational thinking can have dire—even cata-strophic—consequences for the organization.

The purpose of this chapter is to examine the group dynamics that impact board decision making. Our discussion will focus on the two classic pitfalls of group decision making—*Groupthink* and *The Abilene Paradox*—and we will offer strategies that will improve the quality of board decision making. In addition, this chapter offers some practical tools that help to measure and improve the overall perform-ance of boards, along with some strategies to improve the level of director engagement while optimizing board decision making.

WHY WORKING IN GROUPS IS DIFFICULT

Group decision making has long been an important subject of re-search. We can trace research on this topic back to the 1800s, when the renowned French sociologist Emile Durkheim famously asserted that the "mentality of groups is not that of individuals." Durkheim was referring to "mob mentality" and his concerns over the lack of rational decisions made by groups.[1] Influenced by Durkheim, Sigmund Freud also found that the feelings of a group, any group, were always "simple and exaggerated." Freud stated that groups could only experience love or hate, and were unable to live in the "grey" of ambiguity and complexity.[2] In his seminal book *The Crowd*, Gustave Le Bon asserted that ". . . in the collective mind the intellectual aptitudes of the individuals, and in consequence their individuality, are weakened. The heterogeneous is swamped by the homogeneous, and the unconscious qualities obtain the upper hand."[3]

Modern researchers have conducted numerous studies to illus-trate the often negative and counterproductive aspects and outcomes of group decision making. One of the most famous studies, which has since been replicated many times, was that done by Solomon Asch in 1952.[4] Asch demonstrated the impact that group norms have on conformity behaviors, demonstrating that individuals operating in a group setting take more extreme positions than they would if they were alone. His famous research asserts that individuals would knowingly commit errors and agree with the larger group as a result of perceived conformity pressure. More recently, research by Cass R. Sunstein and Reid Hastie has confirmed these original findings by illustrating that groups often not only take more extreme positions than they would if they were acting alone but also fail to achieve any sense of "synergy," because they fail to aggregate their collective knowledge when making decisions.[5]

Factors to Consider

There are several factors that contribute to the overall culture and group dynamics of the board, including the size, cohesiveness, and diversity of the board (see Figure 5.1). Each will be discussed as it relates to group decision making in the boardroom.

Size

The average S&P 1000 board size is approximately ten directors. Obviously, the size of the board varies based on a number of factors. What is critical to remember is that a trade-off occurs from a group dynamics perspective when the size of the board increases. "Social loafing" is the concept used to describe a common and less-than-optimal

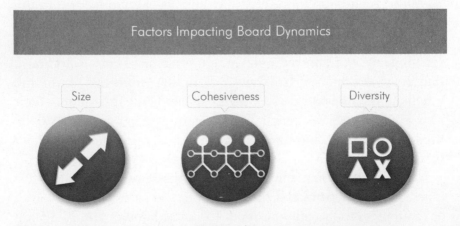

Figure 5.1 Factors Impacting Board Dynamics

aspect related to group decision making: *as the size of the board increases, individual director engagement and participation decreases.* This is not unique to boards, and it's not personal; it just is. This finding, sometimes referred to as the "free-rider tendency," is a natural outcome of group behavior. As the size of the group increases, members believe that "someone else" will know more or do more to provide a solution, suggestion, or recommendation to a given issue. As previously stated, there are many and diverse reasons for increasing the size of a board. You need to carefully weigh those advantages, however, with the very real dangers posed by this phenomenon.

Board Cohesiveness

Board cohesiveness refers to how committed the directors are to each other and to the organization they serve. Not surprisingly, as group cohesiveness increases, so too does productivity, performance, and, in a reinforcing cycle, director engagement. Boards that suffer from a lack of cohesiveness often have developed a *Detached* or *Dependent Culture*, in which members have different agendas, ambiguous goals, or are part of a board that is too large in number. Several factors, such as frequent interactions, getting together outside the boardroom (either socially or on-site at a plant or facility location), and a clear goal or challenge can increase a sense of cohesiveness and, in doing so, create a more *Dynamic Culture*. Sometimes a common enemy, such as a hostile takeover bid or a competitor, will also facilitate a rapid sense of cohesion.

Importance of Diversity

Diversity is the third factor that informs and impacts group decision making. Diversity in every sense—race, gender, skill set, experience, opinions, and perspectives—will help ensure that your board matches the complexity and diversity of the global marketplace. A note of caution: diversity and heterogeneity often lower performance in the short term. When directors see things differently or don't feel that they are "on the same page," there is a lag in performance. However, over time these differences move from being tolerated to being appreciated, and they help boards make thoughtful, reasoned decisions in an increasingly complex and diverse global economy.

Decision making is common to every group whose members attempt to work collaboratively together, as we pointed out in the previous chapter, and how well (or poorly) a group coalesces has a lot to do with its unique culture. Culture ultimately determines the degree of communication, the level of director engagement, and the quality of decision making. Boards with culture problems generally fall into one of two extreme categories:

- *Detached*—cold and angry
- *Dramatic*—warm and friendly

These two distinct and very different cultures result in two very different dynamics and processes, but they ultimately lead to the same outcome: a bad decision.

How a board arrives at a decision, however, is distinct. *Detached* cultures facilitate conflict—passive and aggressive—and a board's inability to manage this conflict often results in the dysfunction of "Groupthink." Boards with a *Dramatic Culture*, in which the culture is warm and friendly but lacking in candor, are often unable to manage their agreement and suffer from "The Abilene Paradox." The travel routes of *Groupthink* and *The Abilene Paradox* are very different, but the destination—a poor decision—is the same.

GROUPTHINK: MANAGING CONFLICT IN THE BOARDROOM

Boards that have devolved into an angry or apathetic *Detached Culture* exhibit *Groupthink* behaviors, as noted by Yale University's Irving L. Janis. In general, *Groupthink* occurs when groups are frustrated and ineffective in managing conflict, so they focus on pressuring members to "get with the program" or "be a team player."[6]

A *Dramatic Culture* is characterized by the exact opposite group dynamics. In this culture, conflict and candor are replaced by warm agreement and self-censorship. Unfortunately, both cultures guarantee poor decision making, since the false consensus exhibited by a *Dramatic* culture leads the board to take inappropriate actions. This false consensus, characterized as *The Abilene Paradox* by Jerry B. Harvey, leads to the same result: a failure to communicate and to solve problems effectively.[7]

That's why a board's independent director and the CEO must understand these group dynamics and ensure that neither dynamic—*Groupthink* or *The Abilene Paradox*—has any influence on high-risk decisions that are critical to the success of the organization. Here are classic examples of *Groupthink*, and Figure 5.2 summarizes the subtle differences between *Groupthink* and *The Abilene Paradox* in board decision making.

CLASSIC EXAMPLES OF *GROUPTHINK*

Classic examples of *Groupthink* from history include the Bay of Pigs Invasion and NASA's decision to launch the Challenger in 1986.

Bay of Pigs Invasion

The chain of events leading up to the failed Bay of Pigs invasion of Cuba in 1961, in which U.S.-trained and equipped soldiers attempted to overthrow Fidel Castro, is a classic example of *Groupthink*. President Kennedy wanted to overthrow Castro, and his subordinates knew it because he inserted himself directly into the deliberations. As a result, his "group" was not thinking rationally or objectively. Instead, the members of his "group" jumped to conclusions, self-censored, and jumped to recommendations that almost led to conflict with the former Soviet Union.

1986 NASA Challenger Tragedy

Prior to the launch of the Challenger in 1986, Morton Thiokol engineers, who were responsible for manufacturing the O-rings for the booster rockets, expressed concern about the O-rings sealing quickly enough at the predicted lower temperatures. NASA administrators applied direct pressure on the engineers to recommend a launch, based on perceived media pressure due to recent delays. Although the engineers had serious concerns, they gave in to the pressure and recommended the launch.

Dysfunctional Board Decision Making
Groupthink and The Abilene Paradox

Boards that are Detached or Dependent are often unable to manage their conflict and, as a result, are victims of Groupthink. On the other hand, boards that are Dramatic or Dependent are often unable to manage their agreement, and, as a result, suffer from The Abilene Paradox. The figure below identifies the culture and likely group decision-making outcome:

Decision-making Dysfunction	Common Attributes	Outcome
Groupthink	Ineffective communication Actual pressure to conform	Inability to manage conflict
The Abilene Paradox	Ineffective communication Perceived pressure to conform	Inability to manage agreement

Figure 5.2 Pitfalls in Board Decision Making

UNDERSTANDING AND AVOIDING *GROUPTHINK*

In 1972 Irving L. Janis identified *Groupthink* as a mode of thinking that occurs when a group's strong desire for cohesion and unanimity prevents it from realistically appraising other alternatives or options. Oftentimes, conformity or peer pressure ensues so that any group member who voices dissent is quickly reminded that the group norm is consent.[8]

Eight symptoms of *Groupthink* have been identified, so the more of these characteristics that exist in a boardroom, the more likely it is that the board will be a victim of *Groupthink*.

1. **An Illusion of Invulnerability:** The board believes that it is invincible and can do no wrong, and past "wins" are often cited as proof of future success.
2. **Rationalizing Valid Concerns and Warnings:** The board makes a collective effort to minimize or rationalize warnings that run counter to the board's desired outcome.

3. **Belief in the Group's Inherent Morality:** The board has an unquestioned belief that it holds the "moral high ground."
4. **Stereotyped Views of Outsiders:** The board views external voices as enemies who have little or no value to add because they are "outsiders."
5. **Direct Pressure Exerted on Members to Conform:** The board as a whole provides direct peer pressure on members who voice dissenting views or opinions.
6. **Self-censorship of Individual Beliefs and Feelings:** Individual board members begin to self-censor their true beliefs and feelings that run counter to the norm of consensus.
7. **Self-appointed "Mind Guards":** Individual board members actively block or withhold outside information that could contradict the current path of consensus.
8. **Shared Illusion of Unanimity:** Individual board members falsely perceive that everyone is in agreement and that there is unanimous consensus.

The process of *Groupthink*, if identified and acknowledged, can be managed and even avoided if boards are willing to have an open, honest dialogue about the issue. Recognition and acknowledgment are key first steps, but alone they are not enough to prevent *Groupthink*. The following suggestions are some effective ways of preventing *Groupthink*:

- Assign members the role of critical evaluator or "devil's advocate," especially to assess their own proposals and recommendations.
- Engage external experts (e.g., CFOs, industry experts, etc.) to provide critical reactions and environmental context.
- Set up another independent group to study a pressing issue and to consider both the group's assumptions and recommendations.
- Periodically break the group into subgroups in order to address process issues within the larger group.
- Take the time to study the larger context within which the group is operating, including conducting board and director assessments.

GETTING PAST *THE ABILENE PARADOX*

Jerry B. Harvey challenged the notion that poor decision making is always the result of *Groupthink* in his seminal 1974 article, "The Abilene Paradox: Mismanaged Agreement." According to Harvey's research, groups don't always make poor decisions because of peer pressure. Instead, Harvey wrote, groups often make poor decisions due to a failure of individual members to communicate honestly and directly with each other.[9]

To illustrate his point, Harvey used both historical examples (such as the Nixon-era Watergate debacle) and personal examples to illustrate the principles of *The Abilene Paradox*. For example, he described a four-hour car trip in 104-degree weather from Coleman to Abilene, Texas (hence the name of the paradox), with his new wife and in-laws in a car with no air-conditioning, all to eat a bad dinner in a cafeteria. His observation later that evening was that no one, not even his father-in-law who had suggested they go to Abilene, really wanted to go, yet no one said anything as the road trip disaster unfolded. Below are some boardroom examples of this paradox.

The Abilene Paradox in the Boardroom

1. Directors agree in a private (not a public) forum about the nature of the situation and what they want to do about it.
2. Directors fail to accurately communicate their thoughts, feelings, desires, and/or beliefs to each another in a group setting. This requires the director to self-censor his or her true beliefs and feelings in order to "go with the flow" or "get on board" with the board.
3. Invalid and inaccurate information leads board members to make collective decisions that are contrary to their individual opinions and views.
4. The board "agrees" on a decision or course of action based on faulty information that no director privately supports.

5. Board members experience frustration, anger, irritation, and dissatisfaction over poor decisions that range from less than optimal to disastrous.

Harvey remarked that it is "pretty absurd isn't it, people taking actions in contradiction to what they really want to do?" Yet, most of us can cite more than a few examples of this group decision-making process occurring. Harvey eventually identified the psychological and group dynamic principles that enable *The Abilene Paradox* to occur, as listed below:

1. **Action Anxiety:** One of drama's most famous characters, Hamlet, famously mused, "To be or not to be, that is the question" as he pondered suicide. Action anxiety occurs when we are unsure of which action to take; we often shut down and do nothing.
2. **Negative Fantasies:** Negative fantasies are the dire, predicted outcomes we mentally construct that provide a basis and justification for not speaking up or not dissenting with the board. Such fantasies often range from thinking that we may be ostracized from the board to fearing we may not be renominated.
3. **Fear of Separation:** A primal, existential fear of being alone, being separated from others, often motivates us to "agree" to a course of action in a group setting when we privately have concerns or misgivings about that course of action. As Harvey correctly illustrates, giving in to this fear often leads to experiencing what Viktor Frankl referred to as "paradoxical intent" and what he called a "paradox within a paradox": the more we fear anything, the more likely we will experience it, including separation.
4. **Real Risk:** Real risk is at play when a board member departs from the board or group norm of agreement. Harvey referred to this risk as the "price of admission" for being human and acknowledged that sometimes the fear of being ostracized, of not being a team player, or of not being renominated must be

weighed accurately and objectively when deciding to voice one's true opinions.

Diagnosing *The Abilene Paradox*

As with *Groupthink*, there are recognizable symptoms of *The Abilene Paradox* that, once identified, can be managed. Harvey recommends the following norms and "ground rules" to help groups, and boards, avoid *The Abilene Paradox*:

- Establish and reinforce the norm of collegial candor, not politeness.
- Treat conflict as not only normal but also necessary, in order to make optimal decisions and to achieve synergy in a board setting.
- Establish the ground rule that everyone must participate and that total engagement in the process is not only expected but also required.
- Avoid being insulated. Bring in "outsiders" from time to time to provide expert input and analysis.
- Don't rush making a major decision. Time is a reflection of priorities; when a major decision, such as strategic direction or succession planning, is in order, take the necessary time to reach a reasoned and thoughtful decision.

As you consider your board dynamics and group decision-making effectiveness, it may be helpful to review the matrix shown in Figure 5.3. Based on the leadership style and group culture descriptions in the previous chapter, you can begin to predict which, if any, decision-making dysfunctions your board may be susceptible to, or is experiencing, right now.

Starting with the leadership style of the CEO, you can begin to reflect on the impact that he or she may be having on your board's culture and dynamic. If the CEO is more *Actualized* and, from a "Big 5" personality perspective, more "Agreeable," then you likely have open discussions in which candor and collegiality abound. However, if your CEO's style is more micromanaging (*Achiever* >

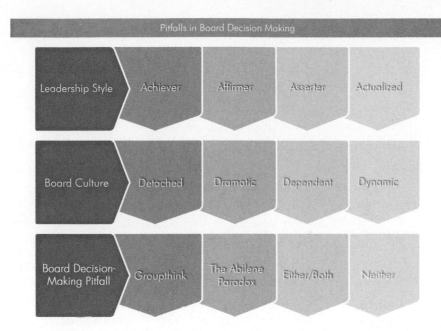

Figure 5.3   The Leadership, Culture, and Decision-Making Matrix

Detached > Groupthink), more accommodating (*Affirmer > Dramatic > Abilene Paradox*), or more controlling (*Asserter > Dependent > EITHER Groupthink OR Abilene Paradox*), then your board is more likely to suffer from group decision-making dysfunction.

Optimizing Board Decision Making

Even if your board has a *Dynamic* and effective culture, you must be vigilant to ensure that your board makes optimal decisions. The goal is to ensure that there is high-quality discussion, with a blend of candor and collegiality, a strong sense of engagement and connection to the business and to each other, and an intentional effort to maximize the collective wisdom of the directors to enhance and improve board decision making. In addition to the specific suggestions already provided for addressing common dysfunctions in board decision making, following are broad steps that your board can take to ensure that it is making sound, reasoned, and rational decisions.

- **Ensure That Everyone Participates:** Invite participants who are less vocal to lead or start certain discussions. Create a norm in the boardroom of going around the table to solicit input and to make sure that everyone expresses his or her true opinion.
- **Silence the CEO:** Many CEOs—some unknowingly, and others on purpose—discourage debate and disagreement by stating their positions and views early in a discussion. Research clearly demonstrates that when leaders speak last, they create more "space" for open dialogue and candor.
- **Reinforce Candor, Not Politeness:** It's nice when everyone gets along, but that type of culture can also create trouble. Develop a norm of authentic candor where constructive conflict becomes a healthy means to a better end, including thanking or otherwise reinforcing the board members who bring up difficult topics.
- **Test Assumptions:** Board members often share so many common traits and values that it is easy for them to develop and act on assumptions. Effective boards test their collective assumptions from time to time by asking "what if" questions.
- **Appoint a Devil's Advocate or Contrarian:** By formally appointing someone to play devil's advocate, you effectively give the director "permission" to challenge the group, propose alternative courses of action, and identify faulty logic or assumptions in a proposed course of action. This technique can be very effective, and the position should be rotated among board members.

Successful boards require the wisdom, energy, and collective synergy that come from highly engaged board members operating as a team. Regardless of the success or sophistication of any particular director, the common pitfalls associated with group dynamics and board decision making must be identified and managed effectively. Structure, process, and procedures can and do help improve communication and decision making. However, it is important to remember that boards are social systems and thus susceptible to human failings, such as self-censorship and detachment, which often occur in group settings. Boards that manage their process dynamics and culture will be better able to fulfill their responsibilities to shareholders, customers, and employees by avoiding *Groupthink* and "trips to Abilene," through better decision making and synergy.

CHAPTER SUMMARY

This chapter examined the group dynamics that impact board decision making by focusing on two classic pitfalls of group decision making: *Groupthink* and *The Abilene Paradox*. It offered strategies to improve the quality of board decision making, along with some practical tools to help measure and improve the overall performance of boards. The chapter also provided strategies to improve the level of director engagement while optimizing board decision making.

WHAT'S NEXT?

Chapter 6, "Board Structure and Schedule," provides some practical guidelines to help determine a board's size and structure, when and how to meet, along with some tips on scheduling successful board meetings.

BOARD STRUCTURE AND SCHEDULE

What's in This Chapter?
- Determining Board Size and Structure
- Frequency of Meetings and Required Preparation
- Board Committees and Practices
- Scheduling Board Meetings
- Chapter Summary and What's Next

In many ways, the corporate board of a publically traded company is the ultimate "free agent." Although it's true that corporate boards do have an absolute set of fiduciary duties and expectations that they must attend to, ranging from approving operational motions and statutory filings to a careful scrutiny of a company's annual plans and budgets, it is also true that there are no hard-and-fast, industry-wide guidelines that govern the execution of these duties. For that matter, boards are not bound by any specific guidelines regarding the number of members or number of meetings that they must have or any rules on the mix of talents, skills, and backgrounds that are required for optimal efficiency and productivity.

This lack of hard-and-fast, industry-wide guidelines is both good and bad news for those serving on a corporate board. The good news is that boards do have wide latitude to set the number of directors at whatever count they wish and to establish their own ground rules for conducting business using the most efficient processes and procedures. The bad news is that this same gift of freedom makes it difficult for the board to know when it "gets it right." This is the question that we address in this chapter—and frankly, this book— how to "get it right."

This dichotomy was noted recently by David L. Larcker and Brian Tayan in their 2013 *Stanford Closer Look Series* article, "Where Experts Get It Wrong: Independence vs. Leadership in Corporate Governance":

> *While there is evidence that governance processes are critical to success—such as proper risk management or a workable CEO succession plan—it is the quality with which processes are designed and implemented rather than as the mere presence of a program that determines whether they will be successful.*[1]

Put another way, the most successful boards use this freedom to construct specific on-the-ground processes that add value to the company and help it to fulfill its fiduciary duties effectively. This chapter tackles the issue of creating an optimal board structure and schedule, and in so doing we address the following topics:

- Board Size
- Meeting Requirements and Preparation
- Effective Committee Service
- Board Scheduling Tips

BOARD SIZE

The average size of a typical S&P 500 board—about 10.8 members— has remained remarkably stable over the past ten years, as reported in Spencer Stuart's 2014 Board Index.[2] Depending on the industry, company size, and past practices, board membership ranges from as large as twenty or more to as small as five or six. As we noted in this chapter's opening comments, the number of serving board members is a completely open question, but like most decisions, there can be both intended and unintended consequences, depending on the choice of an either exceptionally large or small board.

For example, a large board may provide the desired range of expertise and experience, but along with increasing size, a set of more complex dynamics in relationships between board members emerges. This is especially true when membership exceeds ten or eleven members. The lead director also faces greater challenges when ensuring full participation and real consensus among members as the size of the board increases. Still, there are circumstances in which a larger board membership is required, as in the case of a more complex business, such as a large financial institution or a highly regulated company (e.g., an energy company). In these cases, a large board may be needed to fill additional committees in order to satisfy specific regulations or to meet the board's due diligence mandate.

The focus on board size and membership may seem mundane or even a prosaic use of a board member's valuable time, but the decisions made about size, mix of skills, and overall committee structure will have a significant impact on a board's success and productivity, and the fulfillment of its fiduciary duties.

The issue of board composition and the best skill mix will be addressed in greater detail in Chapter 9, "The Other Succession Challenge: The Board of Directors," but it is important to note that the issue of board size and composition should be front and center during every board transition.

MEETING REQUIREMENTS AND PREPARATION

Most large companies require formal in-person board meetings between four and six times a year. General Electric and United Technologies each require eight scheduled board meetings per year according to their proxy material, while Proctor & Gamble requires seven scheduled meetings per year. Again, as noted in Spencer Stuart's 2014 Board Index, S&P 500 companies met on average 8.1 times in 2013; however, it should be noted that this number included any extraordinary additional in-person or telephone meetings to address such matters as acquisitions, divestitures, or contact with an activist shareholder.[3]

Although it might appear that six or even eight formal board meetings a year is a reasonable schedule for the chief executive officer (CEO) and the CEO's team to manage, it's the "behind the scenes" activities that make even four annual meetings a "full-plate" commitment for everyone involved in preparing for, and participating in, these meetings.

What is often forgotten by both board members and even those who are critical of a board's performance is the amount of time that it takes management to prepare for presentations in front of a board and its respective committees. After all, the CEO is meeting with his or her bosses, who determine not only the CEO's compensation but also how long the CEO will stay in office. No one goes into such meetings unprepared. Preparation is especially critical, because any question that a board member might ask, whether it is about an issue related to acquisitions or mergers, or about a significant strategic issue such as cyber security, is based on years of experience and deep knowledge. Looking foolish or uninformed about a particular issue or set of facts in front of the board is simply not an option.

The consequence of this pressure to perform is that a significant amount of time and energy is invested in rehearsal and practice to arrive at a "carefully rehearsed spontaneity" when responding to the board. It's a process that takes a considerable amount of time and effort by multiple people.

Board Meeting Preparation

Generally, board meeting material is electronically delivered just before or on the weekend leading up to the board meeting. Distribution of the material too early risks that the material won't be fresh in the board members' minds during the meetings, and delivery of material that is too late risks the possibility that board members won't have sufficient time to prepare for the board meeting.

The ability to deliver board materials electronically up to the last minute, despite the positive aspect of currency, also adds another complication to the process. Updated material that's delivered on the fly may have the unintended impact of leaving some members unprepared to fully participate in the meeting. As a guideline, board materials should always be sent within a time frame that allows members sufficient opportunity to read and understand the information. In practical terms this means that board material is normally sent out one or two days before the weekend prior to the week in which the board meeting occurs.

As noted earlier, rehearsal and practice are necessary for the management to develop "carefully rehearsed spontaneity" when answering questions based on board meeting materials. Arriving at this polished state of understanding does take time and effort, so time the sending out of materials accordingly.

The Realities of Preparation

Large companies that require more than six formal meetings a year often have specific staff dedicated to the preparation of board meetings. Such arrangements reduce the time that management spends on these meetings and frees them up to focus on important business activities, that is, spending time with customers, clients, employees, investors, and shareholders, and building relationships for possible acquisitions, mergers, or other strategic matters.

Even with the help of a board meeting staff, supplemental meetings will still be required that demand careful preparation by senior management. It is no trivial matter to decide how many of these formal meetings are best suited for a particular company's board. That's why companies often employ carefully considered meeting frequency and timing strategies to maximize the opportunity to deliver on important company operational requirements, such as producing approved quarterly results from the audit committee or approving quarterly 10Q or 10K documents required by the Securities and Exchange Commission (SEC). Such regulatory activity may require the audit committee to meet separately from the formal board meeting (normally by phone) up to eight additional times each year.

Some boards have revised their board schedules to better coincide with these audit committee responsibilities in order to avoid the need for the additional committee meetings and thus reduce workload. Still, committee work often requires input or even approval from the larger board membership, and these responsibilities add to the time required of members.

For example, a member of the senior management team usually works closely with the chair of each committee to prepare for a meeting either in person or by phone. This usually means a review of the agenda to obtain the committee chair's approval as well as a "review of all the material intended for a committee meeting." Once again, this task is critical to prepare for the meeting in order to avoid the appearance (and embarrassment) of being unprepared for questions or unable to give meaningful input.

How Many Committees Are Needed

Unlike many areas of board structure, committee structure does have specific requirements, provided by the New York Stock Exchange Listed Company Manual. The stock exchange listing requirements explicitly call for these standing committees, described below, respectively, in sections 303A.04, 303A.05, and 303A.07:

- Listing companies must have a nominating/governance committee composed entirely of independent directors.
- Listed companies must have a compensation committee composed entirely of independent directors.

The audit committee must have a minimum of three members. All audit committee members must satisfy the requirements for independence set out in Section 303A.02.a.

ABOUT EXECUTIVE COMMITTEES

It's quite common for a board to have on executive committee normally consisting of the nonexecutive chair, presiding director, or lead director, whatever their structure, and the

(continued)

(*continued*)

chairs of the three required committees and the CEO. Before the events of 2001–2002, many boards found that the executive committee, particularly in the case of large boards, had turned into a board within a board (not a good idea). In those circumstances, the full board was asked to vote on issues recommended by the executive committee before the board members had a good opportunity to fully understand and debate the issues before them.

What has developed since that time is the utilization of the executive committee by exception to meet or convene between formal board meetings, acting, for example, as a pricing committee for a new issue of corporate debt. Under these circumstances, the board votes to empower the committee to act on its behalf.

A review of proxies that notes how often committees meet will generally show few if any meetings of the executive committee. In this new world of board governance, it's important that the full board be engaged on virtually every issue facing the board and the company. Conference calls make it possible and should be used between meetings, including extraordinary items to include and engage the full board.

According to Spencer Stuart's 2014 Board Index, companies average 4.2 standing committees. Seventy percent of companies have at least four committees, and 14 percent of companies have six or more committees. Some of these additional committees focus on topics such as finance, safety, health and environmental affairs, innovation and technology, corporate social responsibility, and/or risk.[4]

One of the challenges of multiple committees (more than four) is the requirement for more board members to fill out the committee assignment; generally three or more committee members are needed to take advantage of the dynamic give-and-take and opinions voiced by members. Another challenge is scheduling time for four or more committee meetings in order to allow sufficient time for the committees to fulfill their obligations.

When major strategic and structural change occurs, including a significant acquisition, a major merger of equals, or dealing with a cyber attack, the response is often to establish an ad hoc committee to address the specific issue at hand. Once the issue is resolved, the board must decide if it makes sense to continue the ad hoc committee, so when these special committees are formed, a board should carefully consider both their creation and dissolution.

Committees of the Whole

Some boards have found the approach of "committees of the whole" to be a very effective way of managing committee formation and information dissemination. Essentially, this approach requires all board members to serve on all of the committees of the board. Such an approach means that every board member is part of all discussions and debates, whether the topics are compensation matters, audit committee issues, or governance and nominating committee matters, and is therefore fully informed of all board activities. As a result, committee reports to the full board do not require detailed explanations and background in order for action by the full board to take place.

Another benefit of this approach is that board members can spend extensive time together discussing, debating, and approving issues in committee meetings. These meetings allow respective board members to learn how to work together and to develop confidence in the judgment and candor of other board members. This understanding of different styles, logic, experience, and capacity to communicate can be very valuable when the full board is faced with a critical issue, such as a merger, acquisition, CEO successor, or dealing with an activist shareholder.

A variation on the "committee of the whole" approach is to utilize the governance and nominating committee. Its agenda is generally the shortest and least complicated while it covers issues that the full board should address anyway. Companies that utilize this model integrate this committee meeting into the agenda of the full board meeting. The result is a simpler committee meeting schedule while providing another opportunity for all the members of the board to interact with one another.

EFFECTIVE MEETINGS AND SERVICE

Many variations on board schedules exist, and most evolve over time to suit the character of the business, the company, and the culture of the board. What is most important is that both the board and the CEO (along with the CEO's team) develop a rhythm and pattern that allows sufficient time for the critical ongoing discussion of strategy and its execution.

With variations there are basically two different models for board meeting schedules. In the first type of board meeting schedule, members gather at midday, possibly for lunch, followed by committee meetings throughout the afternoon. A board dinner concludes the day. Some boards meet alone with the CEO, while a more typical practice is to include the other members of senior management or individuals who have made or will be making a presentation to the board. With boards that meet formally only four to six times a year, the board needs as much exposure to the members of the management team, including prospective CEO succession candidates, as possible.

A very good and effective practice (although certainly not universal) is for the board to meet alone with the CEO for breakfast early in the morning (7:00 or 7:30 a.m.). A set or specific agenda is not necessary; rather, the breakfast meeting provides an opportunity to have an open, unstructured conversation around what's on the CEO's mind and the minds of the members of the board.

After the breakfast meeting, the regular board meeting begins and concludes around lunchtime. If at all possible, the day should end with an executive session of the independent directors.

Another potential meeting schedule begins with the board's arrival on the evening preceding the day of the board meeting. Dinner is an opportunity for board members to mix with members of the senior management team, although some boards periodically meet alone with the CEO during the dinner.

The next morning is occupied with committee meetings, followed by the full board meeting, which concludes the day. One of the problems with this schedule is that by the end of the day, many board members are looking at their watches, worried about their departure schedules. Under these circumstances, holding an effective executive session of the independent directors can be and is a challenge.

Still other companies follow a different meeting path. For example, one Acuity Brands organizes board meetings that begin with a dinner for all the independent directors, who gather with the CEO, chief financial officer (CFO), and chief operating officer (COO). The meeting structure allows for socializing and catching up on each other's activities, as a preparation for the next day and a half of meetings. The following morning is occupied by simultaneous meetings of the audit and compensation committees.

Lunch, under this meeting structure, is a roundtable conversation and question-and-answer session with the CEO, CFO, and COO, who update the board on the latest developments in the industry and in the company. The afternoon is dedicated to an update and question-and-answer session from business segments or functional department heads in the company.

The dinner allows the board members to engage with those making the presentations and other members of management at their table, with seating assignments that will ensure a good mix of directors and management. The next morning begins with a breakfast with the CEO and the independent directors, followed by the formal board meeting, which is usually completed well before lunch, as most of the business issues already have been addressed.

The bulk of the meeting time is spent on the formal approval of necessary items, including the governance and nominating committee placed on the board's agenda. While such a schedule does require two nights at the company office or an outside company location, it allows sufficient time for board members to understand critical strategic issues and questions, as well as to stay in touch with key members of the management team at many levels.

CHAPTER SUMMARY

No two boards are the same. What works for one board may not work for another. What is important is that a board periodically review how it organizes itself around the size of the board, the mix of skills of the independent directors, and the number of formal meetings that are needed to organize the appropriate schedule. A groove can turn into a rut, so stepping back periodically to assess these structural questions is an important step to ensure that a board can effectively fulfill its fiduciary duties.

WHAT'S NEXT?

Chapter 7, "Assessing Board Performance," outlines the evolution of board assessments, particularly in light of the passage in 2002 of the Sarbanes-Oxley Act and the NYSE's changes that same year to its Listed Company Manual, requiring "nonmanagement directors" to meet separately from the CEO. You'll learn practical ways to customize assessments to better match your company's processes and board culture, along with tips on conducting peer reviews.

Chapter 7

ASSESSING BOARD PERFORMANCE

What's in This Chapter?
- The Evolution of Board Assessments
- Examples of Board Assessments
- Customizing the Assessment Process
- Finding Your Own Best Practice
- Conducting Peer Reviews
- Chapter Summary and What's Next

A snoted in Chapter 1, "The Changing World of Board Govern-ance: How We Got Here," 2002 was nothing short of a water-shed year for board governance practices, mainly due to two events. First was the passage of the Sarbanes-Oxley Act (SOX), which focused on governance activity within corporate boards and audit committees. Second was a significant change in the New York Stock Exchange (NYSE) Listed Company Manual (303A.03), requiring that "non-management directors meet at regularly scheduled executive sessions without management." These changes to governance practices were in direct response to public outrage over corporate malfeasance and greed that had been so unabashedly exhibited by three high-flying corporations at the time: WorldCom, Enron, and Tyco.

This chapter discusses another important 2002 change to the NYSE Listed Company Manual, which requires annual performance reviews of the board and its committees. As provided in Section 303A.09 of the NYSE Listed Company Manual, boards "should conduct a self-evaluation at least annually to determine whether it and its committees are functioning effectively" as well as "an annual performance evaluation of the required committees of the board—Nominating/Corporate Governance, Compensation and Audit." The requirement also called for an assessment (done within the corporation's Compensation Committee Guidelines) of how well the CEO is adhering to the reviewed and approved corporate goals and objectives set by the board.[1]

While this may be a reasonable request on its face, the NYSE Listed Company Manual unfortunately provides no directions as to how the assessment should be conducted, implemented, or administered; nor does it give any guidance on the comprehensiveness of the assessment, what questions should be asked, or what records should be maintained. The guidelines also do not mention or give any guidance on required peer assessments.

THE EVOLUTION OF BOARD ASSESSMENTS

Prior to the 2002 change in the NYSE's Listed Company Manual, few companies conducted annual board and committee assessments. Dayton-Hudson (the predecessor to Target), home improvement retailer Lowes, and Nucor Corporation (the largest U.S. steel producer, based in Charlotte, North Carolina) are exceptions, having implemented these assessments as early as 1990. For these earlier adopters of board assessments, written questionnaires were used, and it was not uncommon for these companies to even share their experiences, forms, and assessment approaches with one another.

However, in general, these and other companies conducting board assessments at the time utilized a questionnaire format that was administrated for the full board by or through the governance and nominating committee, with each of the other committees conducting their own assessments. A chief executive officer (CEO) assessment, if it was done at all, was generally managed by either the compensation committee or the governance and nominating committee. Today boards pursue a wide variety of practices based on each board's perception of what has worked in the past, the shared experience of other board members, or insight gained through board governance seminars and/or the advice of consultants.

Further impetus to focus on these board assessments came in 2009 when the Securities and Exchange Commission (SEC) implemented a rule for proxy disclosures that required boards to expand any disclosures regarding directors' individual skill sets and diversity, and to better describe overall board composition and their board members' qualifications for board service. This disclosure, along with growing activist shareholder pressure for more scrutiny, prompted boards to provide an outline of how they conduct annual assessments in their proxy communications.

Examples of Boards Assessments

Nucor Corporation's proxy is a good example of how many companies now provide their annual assessment disclosure in response to the NYSE's 2009 assessment disclosure directive. In the company's 2014 proxy under the headline, "Annual Evaluation of Directors and Committee Members," appeared the following statement:

> The Board of Directors evaluates the performance of each director, each committee of the Board, the Chairman, the Lead Director, and the Board of Directors as a whole on an annual basis. In connection with their self-evaluation, each director anonymously records his or her views on the performance of each director standing for re-election, each committee and the board of directors. The entire Board of Directors reviews their reports and determines what, if any, action should be taken in the upcoming year to improve its effectiveness and the effectiveness of each director and committee.[2]

What is not required in the disclosure, but still very much part of the process, is the assessment of the CEO's performance in addition to that of the executive chairman.

The 2014 proxy of General Electric (GE) offers further insight into how other companies view and implement their board assessment efforts. In GE's case, the proxy details can be found under the headline, "Evaluation Process," and offers the following explanation of the process:

> *Each year, either the lead independent director or an independent, third party governance expert, interviews each director to obtain his or her assessment of the effectiveness of the Board and committee, as well as director performance and Board dynamics, and then, after discussion with the chair of the GPAC, summarizes their individual assessments for discussion with the Board and committees. [In years when a third party governance expert conducts the interview, the expert will also discuss this with the lead director before submitting them for Board discussion.]*[3]

CUSTOMIZING THE ASSESSMENT PROCESS

One of the tenets of this book—that no two boards are the same—clearly applies to the board assessment process. As the Nucor and GE examples illustrate, companies use a wide variety of assessment practices, and each reflects the values, preferences, and culture of a particular board.

The lack of guidelines provides both an opportunity and a challenge for the board. The opportunity is the potential to create a customized assessment process that works for the board and its culture. The challenge is to not allow any established assessment process to devolve into a state of "just checking the boxes" so that the process no longer addresses fundamental issues or potential governance changes that would improve the effectiveness of board governance.

Where to Start

The best way to approach the topic of creating a process for board assessment is to assume a "tabula rasa" and start from scratch. This can be accomplished by asking a few basic questions, such as the ones below, about the nature of the assessment, the goals and outcomes of the assessment process, and what makes the most sense for the board:

- When should the assessment take place? Should it be an annual questionnaire or some other instrument?
- Who should gather the information? Should a third party or an annual board roundtable discussion be used, during which the performance of the board, the company, and the CEO are discussed?

Many companies rely on an outside law firm or compensation consultant to gather the responses and then return the responses to the company as a report, without attribution.

As we've noted repeatedly, there are no right or wrong answers to these or any other questions about board governance. However, it is important to make sure that the processes created candidly address the necessary tough questions in ways that contribute to the board's ability to fulfill its fiduciary duties. In addition, the focus must be kept on key questions concerning strategy and effective implementation of that strategy, the effectiveness of the CEO, and other essential questions, such as managing any risks to the company.

The questions that the board asks reflect these company-wide concerns both directly and indirectly, in questions such the following:

- Does the board have the right meeting schedule and receive the correct information between meetings and the pre-board-meeting materials?
- Does the board have the right number of directors or the mix of skills, backgrounds, and diversity as appropriate?
- Is the process for the selection of new directors satisfactory?
- Does the board have adequate time to meet with the CEO?
- Are board meetings conducted in a manner that ensures open communication, particularly for a full discussion and timely resolution of issues?
- Is the leadership of the independent directors effective?
- Are the board members adequately prepared for board meetings?

As we described in Chapter 5, "Group Dynamics and Board Decision Making," good board chemistry and board dynamics are critical to effective board performance. If these two factors exist, boards operating within the resulting positive and collaborative atmosphere will get more out of the process. Experience also suggests that a thoughtful, formal, and rigorous approach to board evaluation yields results that are higher quality and actionable.

FINDING YOUR OWN BEST PRACTICE

Our approach for assessing board performance is a combination and also an integration of some of the best practices adopted by companies that we have worked with over the years. Still, boards must determine what process and method best suits their needs without losing sight that it's less about the actual survey or assessment and more about the candid feedback and dialogue that the assessments generate. It is within these performance discussions that true value and insight are gained.

Impact of Board Culture

Board culture, as we've discussed throughout this book, has a big impact on effectiveness. Clearly, a dysfunctional board culture seriously impacts the value of board assessments. Just how much culture impacts communication and decision making is difficult to measure and quantify in any consistent way. That's why we suggest the use of our *Board Culture Profile*, a copyrighted board assessment form that is included in Appendix A. Among other benefits, the model found in Appendix A can help determine if the board is likely to engage in board decision making that is guided by the principles of either "Groupthink" or the "Abilene Paradox" (see Chapter 6, "Board Structure and Schedule," for more information), essentially a "go-along" mind-set or being influence by the phenomenon of false consensus. Our approach focuses on traditional aspects of director engagement and board performance, which we believe are essential to measure and are the ones that provide the greatest insight into the underlying culture of the board. It's an approach that allows directors to quickly get to "the heart of the matter" in a way that facilitates candor, respect, and change. (See the Appendices to find specific questions for assessing board, director, lead director, and committee and CEO performance and effectiveness.)

Conducting Peer Reviews

According to Spencer Stuart's 2014 Board Index, 34 percent of the S&P 500 companies are now conducting individual director evaluations.[4] Steven R. Walker's National Association of Board Directors (NACD) blog on August 28, 2012 reported at the time that 48 percent of the companies responding to his survey included individual director evaluations.[5] Clearly, board assessment is gaining more support and is moving away from the early days of board assessment, when many directors had a difficult time accepting the idea that they would be subject to feedback regarding their perform-ance as a director.

The way peer feedback is conducted varies just as widely as the format and process varies for board assessment. Here is an example of the questionnaire approach (see Figure 7.1), reproduced from Appendix H.

In the example shown in Figure 7.1, the directors assess each other's performance across a list of attributes, statements, and questions. Other directors provide constructive feedback on a wide variety of criteria, including preparation, constructive debate participation, and willingness to take an unpopular position on an issue. In aggregate, the completed profile should provide an informed view on how directors rate each other's performance as a member of the board. As illustrated in the figure, the results are displayed anonymously, without attribution.

If scores or other indications reveal a particular director who is not meeting the performance level of the other directors, it is the responsibility of the lead director and/or the CEO and lead director to meet with and discuss the performance review's results. As we'll discuss in Chapter 9, "The Other Succession Challenge—The Board of Directors," a peer assessment is very helpful in a discussion with an underperforming board member.

Peer Assessment

Please complete this survey by indicating your rating of each Director. Please include written comments in the space provided at the end of the questionnaire. Your comments will be particularly helpful for addressing matters not specifically covered by the questions.

Unacceptable 1 Below Average 2 Satisfactory 3 Above Average 4 Excellent 5

		Dir. 1	Dir. 2	Dir. 3	Dir. 4	Dir. 5	Dir. 6	Dir. 7
1	Regularly attends all board meetings							
2	Comes to board meetings well-prepared							
3	Participates in a constructive and effective manner, contributing to discussions without dominating them							
4	Communicates with candor and tact, helping the board to manage conflict constructively							
5	Exercises independence of judgment when considering issues, even if taking an unpopular position an issue							
6	Encourages other directors to contribute to board discussions, listens to and respects the opinions of others							
7	Makes an effort to know and interact with members of management and fellow board members							
8	Asks questions focused on policy and strategy rather than tactics and details							
9	Gets to the heart of a discussion quickly							
10	I would recommend this Director to serve another term on the board							
	Average Score							

Figure 7.1 Peer Feedback Form

Source: Peter Browning Partners

Other Peer Review Options

Using a third party or the lead director to interview each board member and using a list of performance characteristics does not significantly change the process. Depending on the structure and practice of the board, the full set of assessments once completed can be reviewed by the governance and nominating committee on behalf of the board when that committee is not established as a "committee of the whole" (a board structure in which all board members serve on all committees, as discussed in the previous chapter).

In general, although it is certainly not always the case, the nonexecutive chairman, lead director, or presiding director leads the committee or preferably the entire board in reviewing the outcome of the assessments. These matters are really the purview of the entire board, and a constructive, open written or verbal discussion around the outcome of the assessment should take place and include the board, the CEO, the chairman or lead director, and, if in place, the peer review committee.

CHAPTER SUMMARY

Board assessments have become the norm. As with so many repetitive practices, assessments can turn into "one more process to deal with before the board can turn to more important matters." Although it's true that familiarity "can breed contempt," it is incumbent on the lead director and the CEO to reinforce the importance of the process before it begins. Even more important is for the committee chairs, the lead director, and all of the directors to take advantage of the outcome of the assessments, in particular the open-ended questions and comments. Everyone involved in the process should view these assessments as an opportunity for candid self-evaluation of their practices and behaviors in order to ensure their own adherence to the highest performance standards.

WHAT'S NEXT?

Board members, by definition, have spent their careers achieving well-recognized, hard-earned success as CEOs, CFOs (chief financial officers), or leaders in other fields. It is this demonstrated individual achievement that has brought them to the board in the first place. But how do you maintain a healthy balance between the strongly held opinions of individual members and the need for consensus? Chapter 8, "The Challenge of the Disruptive Director," addresses a common situation that many boards face: how to handle a director whose behavior, practices, or style disrupts the vital board chemistry to such a degree that the director's departure is necessary for the continued functioning of the board.

Chapter 8

THE CHALLENGE OF THE DISRUPTIVE DIRECTOR

What's in This Chapter?
- Disruptive Members a Common Issue
- Removing Board Members
- The Ying and Yang of Conflict
- Five Types of Disruptive Directors
- Dealing with Disruptive Directors
- How Assessments Help
- Chapter Summary and What's Next

I t is not surprising that a gathering of highly motivated, engaged, driven individuals has a built-in potential for disagreement and conflict. After all, board members, by definition, have spent their careers achieving well-recognized, hard-earned success as chief executive officers (CEOs), chief financial officers (CFOs), or leaders in other fields. It is this demonstrated individual achievement that has brought them to the board in the first place.

Maintaining a healthy balance between the strongly held opinions of individual members and the need for consensus in such a group is no small accomplishment. The best and most dynamic boards maintain authentic collegiality, and members have respect for one another while at the same time freely engage in candid debate and constructive disagreement with one other. Serving on such a board with this rare collegial chemistry can be fulfilling, but it can become a draining and frustrating experience when this collegial chemistry is missing.

This chapter addresses an all too common situation that many boards face: how to handle a director whose behavior, practices, or style disrupt this vital board chemistry to such a degree that the departure of that director is necessary for the continued functioning of the board.

DISRUPTIVE MEMBERS A COMMON ISSUE

In their book, *Boards That Lead—When to Take Charge, When to Partner, and When to Lead*, Ram Charan, Dennis Carey, and Michael Useem note that boards often face the challenge of a disruptive member. "In our experience, as many as half of the Fortune 500 companies have one or two dysfunctional directors," the authors assert in their book.[1] We would agree with this assessment based on the popularity of the topic at board governance conferences, in workshop offerings, and in traditional and social media discussion groups that are focused on board governance. This "statistic" is also supported by my experience of serving on the boards of thirteen publicly traded companies over the past twenty-seven years.

How does a board deal with the thorny issue of telling an otherwise smart and successful board member that his or her services will no longer be required? How does the board manage the bruised ego of someone who is not used to failure or to being confronted with the news that his or her behavior or performance has been judged disruptive and unproductive by fellow board members?

"Firing" Board Members Not Simple

Directors are usually elected by their shareholders annually, which is becoming the prevalent practice, or triennially as part of a staggered board to serve as a peer with fellow directors. In either circumstance, boards cannot "fire" fellow directors during the middle of their term.

If a director should leave before the director's term has expired for whatever reason—disagreement with a board decision, health or family challenge—the SEC requires the company to file Form 8K on behalf of the director, explaining the reason for the departure as approved by the director. In almost every case, a disruptive board member transitions off the board in a structured, procedural way.

Although the circumstances that I faced when I had to deal with a difficult or disruptive director are different and the process that we used to address the challenge varied, the outcome was the same: we were able to move the director off the board. Some board members dealt with the news by simply opting not to stand for renomination. Others submitted their resignation, with the face-saving explanation that their responsibilities outside the board had changed in a way that prevented them from continued service. Once the resignation was submitted, the board simply voted to accept the director's resignation. In some cases, disruptive or underperforming members were simply advised by the lead director that they would not be renominated by the governance and nominating committee.

THE YING AND YANG OF CONFLICT

Boards of directors of publicly traded companies are a unique and distinct microcosm. Elected by shareholders to represent their best interests, these highly accomplished, very successful individuals are mostly hyper, type A personalities. In the setting of the boardroom, they are all peers. Still, leadership roles within the board are required, including the selection of a leader for the chairs of various committees and the selection of someone to take on the role of the full board's nonexecutive chair (also known as lead director or presiding director).

Nevertheless, each board member carries the right to a single, all-important, "yes" or "no" vote, no matter how critical the issue or how vigorous the debate is. As in any group, certain members by virtue of their style, personality, or experience endeavor to exercise undue influence when decisions are being made, and it is these members whom boards must work with to encourage more collaborative ways of interacting.

Collegial candor and robust debate is absolutely critical for effective board dynamics and decision making. As discussed in Chapter 5, "Group Dynamics and Board Decision Making," boards without enough conflict may be making poor decisions due to "Groupthink." Boards that constantly seek to smooth over differences and default to agreement may be "on the road to Abilene." One of the key antidotes to both of these dilemmas is a dissenting director who is willing to provide the board with timely information, differing viewpoints, and a healthy way to disagree. We would note that it is not unusual for dissenting directors to have strong opinions, but they should have the critical skill of being able to *disagree without being disagreeable*.

The extreme but wonderful example of an effective dissenter is Henry Fonda in his portrayal of the lead juror in the 1957 Oscar-nominated film, *12 Angry Men*. As the lead juror who is not convinced that the circumstantial evidence presented by the defense is enough to convict a son accused of murdering his father, Fonda must convince nearly all of the other jurors to adopt his point of view. Fonda's character pursues a classic course toward consensus building as each juror slowly changes his mind during the course of the movie.

AN EFFECTIVE DISSENTER

Henry Fonda's character is an example of "an effective dissenter." Board members who are effective dissenters are critical to any board's efficacy when the board is faced with challenging circumstances and issues that require open and honest dialogue to resolve them. Board members must make an effort to learn how to work together and appreciate the differing philosophies, styles, and personalities of the other members. It's this ability to effectively negotiate through disagreement that defines exemplary group dynamics.

The opposite of the director who is an "effective dissenter" is the "disruptive director." Such directors are, as the cliché goes, "often wrong but seldom in doubt" and "never without an unexpressed thought." It is not unusual to find such a personality pursuing his or her point of view with such intensity that the Chairman/CEO and/or lead director is unable to effectively facilitate the meeting. In such situations, over time these directors end up disrupting the rhythm and chemistry of the board, without adding to the quality of the board in any way. The board must decide if such a director is so disruptive to good process and productive outcome that the board would be better off without that director's presence.

FIVE TYPES OF DISRUPTIVE DIRECTORS

Disruptive directors display little of Henry Fonda's sophisticated consensus-building techniques on display in the movie *12 Angry Men*. In fact, such directors generally fit into one of five categories of disruptive directors that unhinge the board's dynamic and/or derail healthy debate and discussion.

- The Dominator
- The Micromanager
- The Expert
- The MIA Director
- The Dinosaur Director

The Dominator

As a director, the dominator is an individual with a supersized ego, whose outstanding career was built on a "larger than life" personality. In general, this is the stereotypical egotistical personality who is outspoken and perhaps even a bit bullying with the other directors. This individual is the classic example of the true "disruptive director" and someone who, as we noted earlier, is "often wrong but seldom in doubt."

The Micromanager

A detail-oriented director is someone who spends too much time "in the weeds" always seeking more data. While these individuals are well intended in their due diligence, too much information can sometimes be as disruptive as too little information. Still, it usually takes time for the board to develop a sense that such a micro-manager is disrupting the flow of the board's conversations and debate. Furthermore, since inquiries for more information usually require additional work by senior staff, these micromanagers soon come to the attention of the company's CEO, who eventually sends some clear communication about the member to the board's lead director.

The Expert

Boards face a wide range of knowledge and informational challenges, so it is not unusual for them to decide that they would benefit from having a specific subject matter expert on their board. For example, a board may decide that it needs expertise on cyber security, Internet marketing, nuclear energy, or doing business in China. Quite often these are very constructive members who serve on a special committee that is formed to deal with a specific issue.

Clearly, the deep experience brought by these members can be helpful to the entire board and the management team. In some circumstances, however, there is a tendency on the part of these individuals to continue to refer back to their area of expertise again and again. It takes time for fellow directors to develop a consensus that the disruption outweighs the value of their expertise. The biggest challenge is that it is quite often easier to live with the behavior than to try to develop a consensus for whether or not to renominate the disruptive director.

The MIA Director

A director who fails to "show up" either physically or mentally is very disruptive to efficient board operations. Whether the absence is physical or of not being prepared for meetings because the director has failed to read the board materials, the MIA director can drain the productivity of an otherwise effective board. In general, the symptoms of the MIA director include not physically showing up for meetings due to his or her own scheduling conflicts (necessitating calling in to the meetings), paying too much attention to a cell phone or an iPad, and not being able to fully participate in the discussion because the director has failed to read pre-board meeting materials. While these members are not disruptive per se to the quality of a particular discussion within the boardroom or committee setting, their lack of participation is a drain on the overall morale of directors who are present.

The Dinosaur Director

The dinosaur director is a long-standing, experienced director whose day of relevance and ability to add value has passed. The challenge of this director is different in that the director is long serving, was undoubtedly effective in the past, but is no longer able to productively and actively engage in committee and board work. Once a consensus begins to develop that, nostalgia aside, a change must be made, then the challenge of what some call the "empty-seat director" must be addressed.

Boards have too much on their plates to not have every board member fully contributing to the board. In this circumstance, suggesting that the member consider retiring, with full recognition given to his or her contributions, is a thoughtful and effective recourse.

These circumstances require great sensitivity and also much interaction between the CEO and/or the lead director and the director in question.

DEALING WITH DISRUPTIVE DIRECTORS

How does a board develop a collective sense that a fellow member is an impediment to the board's progress? The short answer is that it takes time—time for fellow board members to develop a sense that a change is needed, that enough is enough, and that despite all of the individual's experience and wisdom, the group would be better off without the disruptive member's presence on the board.

Usually, the process toward this consensus building begins simply, with one board member asking another if he or she is having similar difficulties with a fellow board member's behavior.

As this one-on-one consensus grows, eventually one of the directors reaches out to the nonexecutive chair, lead director, or presiding director to share the group's concerns. It is very likely that the CEO and the lead director may have already discussed their own concerns about the disruptive director.

Remember that an effective board is an essential management tool for the CEO and the CEO's team, so clearly any particularly disruptive director draws attention from the company's most senior levels. For example, after a board meeting, the management team surely will discuss the board meeting, both its positive and negative aspects, with upper management. A disruptive member is a perfectly appropriate topic for discussion with these company leaders.

HOW ASSESSMENTS HELP

A well-executed annual board assessment will likely reflect any full or brewing discontent concerning a "disruptive director." If the board uses peer assessments such as those suggested in Chapter 7, "Assessing Board Performance," the disruptive director situation has an even a better chance of surfacing. Still, even with the most robust assessment practices, the challenge remains that many directors are reluctant to explicitly criticize fellow directors.

End of the Process

As the situation unfolds, the lead director should seek views and opinions from other board members about the putatively "disruptive director." It takes time to develop a consensus that action is necessary to deal with a disruptive director, but the lead director should have a sense "that the time has arrived." As we pointed out earlier, boards are a group of peers elected by shareholders, so every effort should be made to communicate concerns and to give the disruptive director an opportunity to change. Nevertheless, sometimes taking action is unavoidable.

As a general practice, most boards include in their governance principles some guidance on director resignations. For example, the

Nucor Corporation's "Governance Principles" lists the following guidelines under the headline, "Change in Job Responsibilities":

> *Directors who have a change or termination in their principal employment or have a substantial change in job responsibilities, in each case other than as a result of a promotion by the director's employer, shall promptly tender their resignation for consideration by the governance and nominating committee. The committee shall evaluate the director's tendered resignation to determine whether it is appropriate for such director to continue on the board in light of the changed circumstances and shall recommend to the board whether to accept or reject such resignation.*[2]

Not all directors accept gracefully the news that their services are no longer required, whether that news is a request for them to resign at the end of their board term or the revelation that their renomination won't be supported by the board. It's not a pleasant time for anyone, and it's one of the more difficult jobs of the lead director, since it is the lead director's responsibility to contact each board member to ensure that a consensus exists to move the disruptive member off the board and to advise the disruptive director that his or her resignation is being acted on and why.

CHAPTER SUMMARY

This chapter addressed the all too common situation of disruptive directors whose behavior, practices, or style disrupt vital board chemistry and productivity.

Five types of disruptive directors were discussed, including the Dominator, the Micromanager, the Academic, the MIA Director, and the Dinosaur Director, along with techniques to deal with each type.

In general, a consensus to take action regarding a disruptive director takes time to develop and develops from the ground up, beginning with individual discussions between directors. In many cases the CEO is at least aware of a potential issue with a disruptive director through their interactions with the lead director.

WHAT'S NEXT?

Chapter 9, "The Other Succession Challenge—The Board of Directors," discusses a potential fourth, important focus for corporate boards beyond keeping the right CEO in place, the pursuit of the company's optimal business strategy, and maintaining an up-to-date CEO succession—that is, creating a succession strategy for the board itself.

THE OTHER SUCCESSION CHALLENGE

The Board of Directors

What's in This Chapter?
- Why a Board Needs to Plan for Succession
- Demographics and Board Service Realities
- Enron, the 2008 Financial Collapse, and Dodd-Frank
- Building a Board Succession Plan
- Single-Issue Candidates
- Onboarding a New Director
- The Chemistry Factor
- Chapter Summary and What's Next

We outlined in Chapter 2, "Role of the Board," the three critical questions that a board must address: (1) Does it have the right chief executive officer (CEO)? (2) Does it have a robust succession process and plan that includes agreement on a short-term successor? (3) Does it have the right strategy, and is that strategy being effectively implemented? This chapter adds an important fourth question: Does it have a succession plan for the board itself?

WHY A BOARD NEEDS TO PLAN FOR SUCCESSION

In many ways, a corporate board follows a set of operational principles that mirrors the priorities of the company it serves. In clear terms, high-performing boards have a consistent focus on ensuring that individual members have the relevant skills and experience to meet the current challenges and risks faced by the company.

A February 28, 2015 issue of *IQ Insights* from State Street Global Advisors (SSGA), written by Rakhi Kumar, head of Corporate Governance, addresses this issue directly: "State Street Global Advisors believes that board refreshment and planning for director succession are key functions of the board." The article goes on to further define the key questions that Kumar believes support effective board director succession practices:

1. Does the board have a process in place that requires it to evaluate its performance and the performance of directors on a periodic basis?
2. Does the board assess the expertise and skills among its directors that are desirable or needed in the context of the company's long-term strategy and risk? (The article suggests an ideal board director experience of one-third new-tenured, one-third mid-tenured and one-third long-tenured. This spread of experience allows the company to leverage the experience and institutional knowledge of longer-tenured directors while limiting the downside risk of short-term director turnover.)
3. Does the company have processes in place that help identify upcoming director turnover.[1]

While these are good overall guidelines for thinking about board succession planning, later in this chapter we will offer a more comprehensive succession grid that is aimed at helping boards carry out this critical selection task. But, for now, let's further consider why having a process in place is more important than ever.

DEMOGRAPHICS AND BOARD SERVICE REALITIES

As we're constantly reminded by the popular press and other media, our life span (and, importantly, our healthy life span) has steadily increased in the past twenty-five years. This demographic reality is reflected in many aspects of our lives, from the boom in senior living communities to the number of products and services aimed at this new class of consumers. Our assumptions about living a long life are also reflected in how we plan for retirement. All financial-planning algorithms now assume a ninety-year (or more) life span. More people than ever above the traditional "retirement age" (sixty-five) are participating in marathons and triathlon races, climbing mountains, trekking through the rain forest, starting new businesses, or engaging in a second career.

This general societal desire to be *more* productive later in life rather than *less* productive has, of course, impacted board service. In fact, according to Spencer Stuart's 2015 Board Index, the average age of a board member since 2004 has moved up from 60.5 years old to 63.1 years old.[2] And that's just an average. As a practical matter, our experience tells us that a typical board is just as likely to have a 70-year-old member as a 60-year-old member. That's because the general assumption is that board members are just as effective at 70 or 75 years old (or older) as they were earlier in their career. You might say that the cliché for board service today is that "70 is the new 60."

The "official" retirement policy for board members also mirrors this trend. Most of the S&P 500 companies that have established a retirement age (currently about 73 percent of these listed companies) set the official retirement age at seventy-two years of age or older. Thirty percent of this S&P 500 group set the age of retirement at seventy-five years of age or higher.[3]

ENRON, THE 2008 FINANCIAL COLLAPSE, AND DODD-FRANK

Another set of factors that impacted board retirement guidelines and succession includes the new, heightened scrutiny of boards, their practices, and the continuing stream of proposed board governance changes and responsibilities. Board experience was invaluable as boards had to deal with the requirements of the New York Stock Exchange (NYSE) listing changes, the Sarbanes-Oxley Act, and the challenges of the 2008 financial collapse, followed by the new demands of the Dodd-Frank legislation, particularly "say on pay."

The practical upshot of these changes to board governance is that the responsibilities workload inside boardrooms has greatly increased. Dodd-Frank legislation has brought its own additional requirements. Boards are now faced with deciding whether and when to act on such things as annual elections and majority vote. Proxies have expanded exponentially with requirements for expanded directors' biographies, including descriptions of what value the directors add to the board, governance practices, whom shareholders should contact on the board if they have questions, the duties of the lead director, and the board process for selecting new directors.

All of these additional duties and responsibilities for board members must be fit within an optimal board size of ten members. In fact, the average size of a board (about 10.8 members) has not changed

IMPORTANCE OF REFRESHING BOARD MEMBERSHIP

Clearly, shareholders are going beyond interest in the process that boards follow for board member succession to concerns for such issues as tenure, diversity, and quality of board member assessments. BlackRock, the largest manager of securities in the world, offered the following comments in their recently published "Proxy Voting Guidelines for U.S. Securities":[4]

We encourage boards to routinely refresh their membership to ensure the relevance of the skills, experience and attribute of each director to the work of the board. . . .
We encourage boards to disclose these views on: the mix of competencies, experience and other qualities required to effectively oversee and guide management. . . .

since 2004, according to Spencer Stuart's 2015 Board Index of
the S&P 500 companies.[5]

As a result, board member compensation has increased to under-
write these new responsibilities. For example, the enhanced
audit directive requirements of the Sarbanes-Oxley Act promoted
increases in pay for the chair of the audit committee and its
members. As other responsibilities were added due to the growing
list of statutory requirements, other board committee chairs and
committee members began to receive increases in their compensation as well. Today, the average board compensation for S&P 500
companies is $264,000—up 24 percent from 2009 and up consid-
erably more from 2002 compensation levels.[6]

BUILDING A BOARD SUCCESSION PLAN

Building a board succession plan requires an organized and consistent approach that considers a wide range of relevant factors,
including experience, skills, fitting in with the board culture, and
age. We recommend the use of a grid system (see Figure 9.1), which
is designed to bring all of these factors into a single, clearly understood visual representation.

The matrix in Figure 9.1 places members on a horizontal axis
according to their chronological age beginning on the left and then
moving to the right with the last to retire. The vertical axis lists
critical skills that the board feels are important to long-term effective
performance. The grid makes it easy to see which members might be
retiring next and what skills these members will take with them when
they leave. This is such a good tool once completed that it should be
included as a standard exhibit in the material for the meeting of the
governance and nominating committee. Some companies, such as
United Technologies, that choose to create such a grid use the
information in their proxies as an illustration of the board's diversity
of skills and experience. (See Figure 9.2 for an example.)

Where to Begin

As suggested by the article by Rakhi Kumar mentioned earlier in the
chapter, a reasonable distribution of age and tenure across the board

		Annual Meeting as of which Director is not eligible for re-election					
	2017	2018	2019	2021	2023	2027	2030
Directors	Director 1	Director 2	Director 3	Director 4	Director 5	Director 6	Director 7
Director since	1999	1999	1996	2007	1999	2012	2001
Age as of (date)	71	70	69	67	65	61	58
Board Committees							
Background/ Experience	• Governance (C)	• Governance	• Audit	• Compensation • Audit	• Compensation (C) • Governance	• Compensation	• Audit (C)
Digital/Customer Facing Technology							X
Cyber Security						X	
International	X	X		X	X		
Marketing	X			X	X		
Manufacturing			X	X			
Retail	X	X					X
Human Resources		X			X		
Information Technology				X		X	X
M&A		X	X				
Government/ Govt Relations				X			

Figure 9.1 Board Succession Planning Matrix

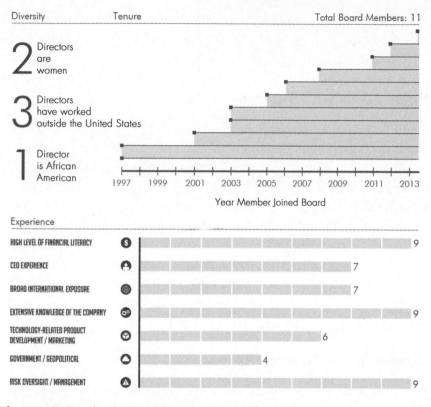

Figure 9.2   The Director Succession Grid

is very desirable. The grid is clearly a useful tool to make this age-range determination easy to visualize and thus to evaluate the loss of important experience and understanding of the company's business, strategy, culture, people, and performance that will be lost with each annual or biannual retirement cycle.

This clear look at the overall makeup of the board should be the starting point for a thoughtful process that allows various committees and the full board to consider what skill set and background would add breadth and depth to the current board's experience and capabilities. This is no small consideration, since you can be sure that shareholders pay attention to this mix. For example, early last year two of Apple's leading shareholders publicly criticized the company because seven of its eight directors were white males over the age of fifty. In response, the company amended its nominating committee charter to demonstrate its commitment to board diversity, subsequently appointing a second female director to fill its next board vacancy.

Board Job Description

Ultimately, the governance and nominating committees and then the board must consider the needed skills for the next director in the form of a "job description" that summarizes the outcome of their considerations. In addition to the raw skills needed, it's important for this process to include the need to create diversity on the board and, importantly, to allow enough time in the process to find qualified candidates. Boards are increasingly concerned with diversity (as they should be), and that has ramped up competition to hire women and people of color with the appropriate background, experience, and qualifications to serve on a board of a publicly traded company.

Single-Issue Board Members

A "single-issue" board candidate is sometimes needed because of an overriding concern or threat to the company, such as data and cyber security, which is an issue that was brought into sharp focus in 2013 and 2014, when cyber criminals hacked into Target and Home Depot customer servers and made off with millions of records containing personal information that could be used to steal the identity of the victims. The threat is so important that the Securities and Exchange Commission (SEC) is asking companies specifically how they plan to address these hacking threats, and Institutional Shareholder Services (ISS) has indicated that it would recommend withholding votes for individual board members, committee chairs, or even the entire board in the event of an obvious failure to address significant risk, such as a major cyber security breach.

It is interesting to note that the January 23, 2015 issue of *Agenda* references a survey conducted by Money-Media, a Financial Times Service Company, which found that 17.7 percent of the respondents said that their boards had enlisted a director with cyber security experience.[7]

Other single-issue candidates might include those with digital retail commerce experience or international candidates, including foreign nationals—that is, individuals from a new or potential market, such as China, India, Brazil, or Russia. Specific industry experience might also be an important selection criterion. For companies working with the federal or military branches of government, it is not unusual for them to seek such background and experience either from the military or someone who has spent considerable time in Washington, DC.

Sometimes this single-issue guidance is specific. For example, after the financial crisis of 2008, activist shareholders pushed for board members with more financial or banking services experience. The 2002 Sarbanes-Oxley legislation noted earlier in this chapter requires that the board designate a financial expert for the audit committee and to certify that the other members of the audit committee are fully qualified to serve on the committee. That's why former or current chief financial officers (CFOs) with an up-to-date understanding of the latest requirements for financial reporting and accounting or retired partners from one of the major public accounting firms are in high demand.

Hire a Consultant?

One option that boards have for seeking advice and guidance in a special area is to hire a consultant on an ongoing basis, especially if the issue is critical to the company, as in the case of cyber security. The preferred option is to hire a full-time consultant, since boards only meet formally four to six times a year and generally over two days, with half of the time taken up in committee meetings. It is possible to bring in a subject matter expert to consult with the members between meetings, but it generally is not nearly as productive or as helpful as hiring a full-time consultant.

The Chemistry Factor

The power of "getting along" (board chemistry), as we discussed earlier in this book, cannot be overemphasized. In fact, it's one of the top items on our list of attributes of board members that creates a highly effective board. As a reminder, these attributes are as follows:

- A group dynamic that balances collegiality with candor.
- A fundamental understanding of the business.
- An appropriate blend of experience, expertise, and wisdom.
- A commitment to invest time and energy into the board and the company.
- A healthy working relationship with the CEO.

The most effective boards develop these attributes, especially the critical component of board chemistry, over time through the often difficult experience of learning the individual styles and personality traits exhibited by the other directors. Building these relationships does pay off. According to a study conducted by Solange Charas, published in the January 9, 2015 issue of the *International Journal of Disclosure and Governance*, "the impact of a board functioning as a team is an eight times greater predictor of corporate performance than individual director's demographics."[8] The basis for this team-work is a collaborative and collegial chemistry that must be built over time. The fact is, the potential for an individual candidate to have the ability to be part of this productive board chemistry cannot be gleaned from reviewing a résumé; it takes time and effort to ensure, beyond what's on paper, that bringing the candidate on board will not result in someone who dilutes, if not harms, a high-functioning board.

The Selection Process

Once an agreed-upon job description is developed, the lead director or chair of the governance and nominating committee asks the board members directly if any members have suggestions for candidates either through personal association or through industry sources. Notwithstanding the identification of a strong, agreed-upon candidate, a list of several candidates should be developed, sorted by preference.

Quite often the results of this process are given to a professional search firm. At the upper end of the scale, the fees of these search firms can reach $120,000 to $130,000, so it is not a trivial matter.

If a potential candidate expresses interest and, importantly, indicates that he or she has the time to fulfill the commitments to the board, the director or the chair of the governance and nominating committee—sometimes with, but often without, the CEO—will hold an in-person meeting with the candidate. If the board is relying on its own generated list of candidates, usually the board member who knows the candidate will make the initial contact, but the lead director or the chair of the governance and nominating committee (depending on how the board is organized) instead may make the initial contact.

Next Step

If the candidate has a satisfactory meeting with the lead director or the chair of the governance and nominating committee and spends some constructive time with the CEO, the consideration of a prospective board member's candidacy generally will be taken up at the next board meeting, before any action is taken or further meetings are held.

The best practice is for the candidate to meet with all members of the board, although this is not always possible. Sometimes the candidate just meets with several other board members. In any event, at the conclusion of this due diligence process, the nominating committee and then the full board recommends and votes to elect the new director.

EDUCATING, ONBOARDING A NEW MEMBER

The last and critically important step in the selection process is the introduction and education process that follows the new member's election to the board. Boards meet on a limited schedule, so it takes time for a member to develop an understanding of the dynamics of the business and get comfortable with its culture. Learning to work with other board members, let alone building a productive chemistry among other directors, takes time.

In the meantime, it is normal practice for the new director to visit the corporate office alone in order to meet with the members of the management team, including the corporate secretary, general counsel, CFO, and other key corporate players. Depending on the business, new board members should also visit relevant stores, plants, and distribution or IT centers to better understand the business from the ground up.

CHAPTER SUMMARY

This chapter discussed an added, but all-important fourth question for boards: Does the board have a succession plan for the board itself?

To set this process in place, the chapter offered a comprehensive way for boards to keep succession a key part of their process, along with a useful succession planning grid that tracks each board member's potential retirement for the upcoming ten years. The chapter also discussed "single-issue" board members and how to best utilize their expertise on a board.

Board chemistry and the ability to work as a team is a critical factor in board productivity, and this chapter discussed ways to ensure a collegial and cooperative mind-set on a board.

Finally, the chapter discussed the selection process for nominating and searching for new board members.

WHAT'S NEXT?

Chapter 10, "What's Next in the Boardroom?," is an honest look at the future of governance, given the influence of recent historical events, societal changes, and legislative and regulatory action, including the 2002 passage of the Sarbanes-Oxley Act and a "game-changing" revision to the NYSE Listed Company Manual that same year. The future of governance practices was also greatly impacted by the 2010 passage of the Dodd–Frank Wall Street Reform and Consumer Protection Act, which was a direct response to the 2008 financial crisis and was designed to improve accountability and transparency in the financial system, and to protect American taxpayers and consumers from both future "too big to fail" bailouts and abusive financial services practices.

Chapter 10

WHAT'S NEXT IN THE BOARDROOM?

What's in This Chapter?
- The Six Biggest Challenges for Boards
- Ongoing Scrutiny of Executive Compensation
- Continuing Demands for More Proxy Information
- More Shareholder and Investor Activism
- Greater Demands for Proxy Access
- Sharper Focus on Risk Management
- Ever-Increasing Scrutiny of Board Composition
- The Way Forward
- Chapter Summary and What's Next

B oards today face unrelenting pressure to provide more information to investors and shareholders. As noted at the beginning of
this book, the changes to governance practice over the last sixty-five
years have been driven by extraordinary events in the business environment as well as unprecedented upheavals in societal norms and expectations. These economic and societal changes include the following:

- A move away from a manufacturing economy that expanded
  during World War II and then dominated the world economy

throughout the 1950s and 1960s until the beginning of today's service-oriented economy.

- Improvements in the manufacturing process during the 1970s and 1980s, particularly the changes related to the introduction of automation that replaced individual workers.
- The diminishing influence and power of organized labor.
- The "creative destruction" of industry in the 1980s and the new business world that it ushered in, dominated by "corporate raiders" and the use of leveraged buyouts.
- The bursting of the dot-com bubble in 2001.
- The blatant corporate malfeasance that was exposed in 2001 and was exemplified by oil and gas trading giant Enron Corporation, communications giant WorldCom, and home security services company Tyco.
- The huge 2008 financial meltdown and the ensuing economic panic that nearly destroyed worldwide financial and banking systems.

Layered on top of the economic and social consequences resulting from these events are new governmental and regulatory agency rules and guidelines that have been imposed on boards and traditional governance practice. These changes included the following:

- The passage of the Sarbanes-Oxley Act in 2002 (also known as the Corporate and Auditing Accountability and Responsibility Act), which was intended to strengthen the integrity of internal reporting requirements. The law was a direct response to the Enron, WorldCom, and Tyco debacle.
- A 2002 revision to the New York Stock Exchange (NYSE) Listed Company Manual requirements, also in response to the Enron, WorldCom, and Tyco debacle that same year, which strengthened board member independence and voting guidelines; set standing committee minimums (audit, compensation, and governance/nominating); called for annual assessments of the chief operating officer (CEO), the board itself, and each of the three standing committees; and, importantly, set a requirement that the board's independent directors must meet

periodically in executive session without company management being present.

- The July 2010 passage of the Dodd-Frank Wall Street Reform and Consumer Protection Act (which was a direct response to the 2008 financial crisis), which was designed to improve accountability and transparency in the financial system, and to protect American taxpayers and consumers from both future "too big to fail" bailouts and abusive financial services practices.

As a result of these key historical events and societal, governmental, and regulatory responses to them, the future of governance is likely to be dominated by six key trends in the coming years:

1. Ongoing scrutiny of executive compensation.
2. Continuing demands for more proxy information.
3. More shareholder and investor activism.
4. Greater demands for proxy access.
5. Sharper focus on risk management.
6. Ever-Increasing scrutiny of board composition.

ONGOING SCRUTINY OF EXECUTIVE COMPENSATION

Chapter 1, "The Changing World of Board Governance: How We Got Here," offered a wide-ranging discussion of CEO compensation and the major historical factors that underpin the current discussion of this issue. As we noted, an historic low point in CEO compensation was reached in 1970, when the average wage gap between the CEO and a typical worker was pegged at a factor of only twenty-five. The gap has widened steadily ever since. During the 1980s merger and acquisition frenzy, the wage gap greatly increased, especially in response to that decade's focus on long-term strategic planning that tied ever-increasing compensation packages to targeted CEO performance.

By the late 1980s, the gap was enough of a concern to prompt attempts at federal regulation that was designed to curb CEO wage inflation. One impetus for this regulatory attention was the unintended consequence of urging companies to use stock options in lieu of cash for both short- and long-term compensation, resulting in even wider gaps throughout the 1990s. Throughout the dot-com boom, the wage gap continued to grow so that by 2004 executive pay was on average 104 times that of the average worker, with the top 10 percent of executives earning at least 350 times the pay of an average worker.

Legislative and cascading regulatory responses to Enron, World-Com, and Tyco's corporate malfeasance in 2002 (the Sarbanes-Oxley Act), and to the high-risk banking practices that resulted in the 2008 worldwide financial crisis (Dodd-Frank Act) have also tried to confront the issue of CEO compensation.

Pressure to Address CEO Pay

The biggest change that has occurred in the last decade as a result of legislative action is the implementation in 2011 of Section 951 of the Dodd-Frank Act, requiring a mechanism to be set up for shareholders to have input into decisions about CEO compensation, known widely as "say on pay."

Essentially, "say on pay" is a way for shareholders who are unhappy with a CEO's compensation to express their discontent through voting "no" on the appropriateness of how much a company's CEO is being payed. Companies can choose whether to include this "say on pay" option in their proxy material annually, every two years, or every three years. Most companies choose the annual option.

Up until the implementation of Section 951, shareholder resolutions concerning CEO pay had been placed on proxies sporadically, where they garnered limited support. As a matter of reference, in 2006 only five companies received such proxy proposals.

Pay for Performance

The Securities and Exchange Commission (SEC) recently released a "Pay for Performance" disclosure rule (expected to be finalized in late 2015) that will require companies to disclose the relationship between the compensation paid to named executive officers (NEOs) and the financial performance of the company. This information will be included in the Compensation Discussion & Analysis

(CD&A) portion of a company's annual proxy and also satisfies a directive of Dodd-Frank.

As a result of these changes, shareholders will have access to a "Five-year Executive Compensation Table" that includes total CEO compensation along with the average compensation of the company's other NEOs. Another table, known as the "Summary Compensation Table," will set forth total reported yearly CEO and NEO compensation and will include adjustments for equities based on their fair values that vest in the applicable year. The annual change in pension value (based on the actual value of annual service cost) will also be part of the table.

The new SEC rule also requires that companies provide a detailed rationale to support CEO compensation and then correlate that pay level with a peer group's Total Shareholder Return (TSR) and its own cumulative TSR. A multiyear reporting requirement will be phased in in 2016, which will require disclosure of three years of actual paid executive compensation along with this TSR data. Finally, on the horizon is a controversial Dodd-Frank–driven change that is expected to be finalized by the SEC in 2017, which requires a company's proxy to include the ratio of CEO compensation to that of the average company employee.

CONTINUING DEMANDS FOR MORE PROXY INFORMATION

Boards are elected to support and work with the management team in order to deliver long-term shareholder value. No two companies in the same industry, let alone in different industries, employ the same metrics to drive their CEO's desired behavior, particularly as it regards the annual bonus plan. The metrics selected by a management team and approved by the board should reflect the metrics that are felt to be most effective in reaching the company's desired strategic objectives. Slowly but surely, policy requirements as described above are forcing every company to include TSR metrics, with the deleterious effect of making it even more difficult for CEOs to employ their own unique philosophy, style, and approach in order to implement their strategy most effectively.

In addition to more data in the CD&A, since 2002 the SEC has required enhanced disclosures for each director through expanded biographies, more detailed explanations that support board membership, and detailed information concerning the other boards that members have served on in the past five years. In addition, there are new required disclosures on board leadership structure.

Responsibilities Detailed

Proxies must now explain why the CEO is also board chairman and provide a detailed accounting of the responsibilities and requirements of the lead director. If the CEO is not the board chairman, then the responsibilities of the nonexecutive chairman must be fully explained. In addition, proxies must include disclosures about the board's role in risk oversight, explanations of the board evaluation process, up-to-date direct contact information for shareholders, an explanation of the nominating process for board directors, stock ownership requirements for directors, and an accounting compensation for board directors.

Since 2012 proxy rules require affirmation and explanation of the independence and compensation levels of committee members. Similar disclosure requirements are in place for the compensation committee advisors. In addition to all of these disclosures, pressure from certain activist shareholders continues for providing clearer, more detailed information and more graphs (particularly around matters relating to pay).

Recently, on July 1, 2015, the SEC published proposed rules for the implementation of Section 944 of Dodd-Frank, which sets requirements for CEO compensation claw-back rules requiring the recovery of excess incentive-based compensation when the company needs to file an accounting restatement. Final action by the SEC on hedging policy disclosures is still pending.

MORE SHAREHOLDER AND INVESTOR ACTIVISM

Activist shareholder objectives are generally short term, and the actions that they take reflect the current economy and market conditions. For example, in the 1980s, activists either threatened "green mail" or used large amounts of debt in the form of high-yield bonds to effect leveraged buyouts in order to achieve their objectives.

In the 1990s, when stock prices quadrupled, investors of all stripes were more interested in picking winners during the remarkable bull market than challenging boards of directors. Following the dot.com bubble collapse in the late 1990s and as the new millennium unfolded, hedge funds were the activist vehicle of choice to achieve returns well above the market rate. It was a high-returns ride that everyone was happy to join — from large institutional investors to the largest financial institutions and banks — until it all came crashing down in 2008.

As the economy recovered from the 2008 financial crash and resulted in historically low interest rates, activist shareholders, flush with cash from the institutional endowments and pension funds, were now more engaged than ever. As a point of reference, 27 public activist attacks on companies occurred in 2000. In 2014 activists mounted nearly 250 company attacks.

It is important to note that size, level of sophistication, or even performance do not necessarily preclude an activist shareholder publicly attacking a company. Companies such as Apple, Procter & Gamble, Microsoft, PepsiCo, DuPont, and many other well-known companies have experienced the challenge of dealing with activist shareholders' public challenges.

In this environment it behooves any board to take the time to scrutinize the company's performance through the eyes of possible activist shareholders. Activist shareholders' objectives are short term, since they must deliver above-market returns to satisfy their institutional investors. But it does not always make sense to implement or increase a dividend, sell a division, or buy back stock, especially when it means utilizing capital for more strategic, long-term purposes. Certainly, there are underperforming companies in which activist shareholders' demands are well deserved and needed. The challenge is to be sure that your company is not one of them.

In order to answer the challenges proposed by activist shareholders, boards need to be more engaged than ever in the company's strategy and the dynamics of the industry in which they compete, while doing everything possible to compete and outperform their competitors.

GREATER DEMANDS FOR PROXY ACCESS

One of the requirements of Dodd-Frank was more proxy access, which is shorthand for the mechanism that gives shareholders a voice in corporate board elections. It refers specifically to the right of shareholders to place their board director nominees on a company's proxy card if they are dissatisfied with a corporate board. Although the requirement was invalidated by the count in 2011 due to a Chamber of Commerce challenge after being implemented by the SEC, activists continue to propose proxy access for inclusion and a vote in annual proxies.

During 2012 and 2013, only thirty-four shareholder-backed proxy access proposals were included in proxies, with just ten of them receiving the majority support of shareholders. In November 2014 the office of the New York City comptroller launched "the Boardroom Accountability Project" by submitting proxy access proposals for seventy-five companies. These actions were followed by statements from BlackRock, favoring the formula of at least 3 percent of outstanding shares for at least three years for up to 25 percent of the board candidates who are up for election to be placed on the proxy. Vanguard added to the pressure by expressing a preference for a proxy access term of 5 percent per share ownership for at least three years and 20 percent of the board seats. The Teachers Insurance and Annuity Association–College Retirement Equities Fund (TIAA–CREF), a Fortune 100 financial services organization, advised many companies in which it had investments of TIAA–CREF's preference for the 3–3–25 formula, while Calpers, the California State Teacher's Retirement System (CalSTRS), and Institutional Shareholder Services (ISS) also expressed support for the 3–3–25 formula. Excluding shareholder proposals that were not contested by management and proposals voted on in which the company had always adopted a 3 percent proxy access, there were seventy-five shareholder proposals when votes took place; forty-five proposals received majority support, and thirty did not. The numbers speak for themselves. This is an issue that is gaining momentum; it remains to be seen if it will expand to the extent of being an issue for a majority vote and annual elections.

Marc S. Gerber and Richard J. Grossman of Skadden Arps also reported a significant increase in proposals for proxy access in their June 23 2015 article, "Proxy Access: The 2015 Proxy Season and Beyond." And there are other signs that the issue of proxy access is still important to activist investors.[1]

SHARPER FOCUS ON RISK MANAGEMENT

In 2002 the NYSE dramatically changed its requirements for listed companies. The impact of this change has been noted several times in this book, including the most significant one that requires directors to meet separately from the CEO. However, another 2002 change that required the audit committee to meet periodically to consider and assess risks also has had an enormous impact on governance practice.

The impact has been slow to take effect due to at least two years of debates inside and outside boardrooms about how to implement the requirements. During the balance of the decade leading up to 2008, the practice developed of giving annual presentations to the full board, led by the CEO and the CEO's team, about general risks to the company and how they were being managed.

Today, the ever-popular "heat map" displaying risks by size and likelihood of occurrence is widely employed. In the meantime the audit committee continues to address risks concerning the quality and fidelity of the quarterly and annual financial reports. In addition, some companies, particularly large financial institutions, are addressing this requirement by adding a risk committee or by creating a director position of chief risk officer.

Another risk faced by boards is the potential damage of cyber criminals and the need to address cyber security risks. We discussed the well-publicized customer data security breaches at Target and Home Depot earlier in this book.

In 2011 the SEC issued guidelines regarding public company disclosures of cyber security risks. In fact, this is such an important governance issue that Institutional Shareholder Services (ISS) stated that it will recommend withholding votes against either the specific committee or the entire board in the event of a significant failure of risk oversight. The bottom line is that formal risk management by companies, including understanding and addressing cyber security management, is with us to stay. Boards and their committees ignore the issue at their own peril.

EVER-INCREASING SCRUTINY OF BOARD COMPOSITION

In an effort to influence board composition, certain activist share-holders have begun to focus on the issues of board member tenure, diversity, and mix. ISS has indicated that in cases where the average tenure of all directors exceeds fifteen years, it will scrutinize boards for independence from management and to ensure sufficient turn-over in order to allow new perspectives to be added to the boards.

The issue is in its early stage of development, and it remains to be seen whether it will build momentum across a broad cross section of institutional shareholders. BlackRock, in its 2015 Proxy Voting Guidelines for U.S. Securities, devoted a separate section to this issue. The particular issue was that of boards seriously considering their responsibility for refreshing the membership of their boards.

Adding to the chorus, as reported in the July 10, 2015 issue of *Agenda,* in an article titled "Calpers Cautions on Composition Policy,"[2] CalSTRS also released a publication emphasizing its position on board composition.

It behooves the governance and nominating committees, as well as entire boards, to engage in discussion and consideration of the topic, as the issue requires the full board's engagement. No one should overreact, but on the other hand, board members should be aware of the issue and, as openings occur on the board and are filled, understand that scrutiny will follow.

THE WAY FORWARD

As we've outlined throughout this book, the challenges that boards face today are directly connected to relatively recent, large-scale economic and social upheavals that have driven increased restrictive federal and regulatory agency rules and guidelines, and more shareholder scrutiny and activism. We've also noted that some of these changes have a definite political, environmental, or socially focused agenda behind them, including these examples:

- Individual investors, sometimes called "corporate gadflies," who repeatedly file common shareholder proposals at multiple companies.
- Institutional investors with a "social investing" purpose or who are affiliated with a religious group, charitable organization, or public-policy organization.
- Pension funds—chiefly state or municipal public funds or private "multi-employee" funds (e.g., labor unions)—whose representatives advocate for their cause.

The bottom line is that efforts to influence boards and their companies will continue, and in response the SEC is likely to continue to promulgate new requirements.

Of course, what hasn't changed, no matter what the future holds, is the board's fiduciary duties to deliver long-term sustainable value to shareholders. In order to do so, boards need to continue to find ways to constructively, thoughtfully, and legally comply with new regulations and to do what is necessary to address any issues without compromising their ability to spend sufficient time answering the three most important questions that every board must answer:

- Do we have the right CEO?
- Do we have a current, agreed-upon succession plan in place?
- Do we have the right strategy, and is it being effectively implemented?

CHAPTER SUMMARY

The future of governance is likely to be dominated by six key trends that include ongoing scrutiny of executive compensation, continuing demands for more proxy information, more shareholder activism, greater demand for proxy access, a sharper focus on risk management, and ever-increasing scrutiny of board composition.

These trends are the result of historical events and societal changes, and the unique set of governmental and regulatory responses that were offered in response to them. Focus on executive compensation grew more intense as the wage gap between CEOs and the average worker steadily widened through the 1980s and 1990s, and was exacerbated by the Enron, WorldCom, and Tyco corporate malfeasance scandal in 2002 and the worldwide financial crisis in 2008.

Increasing demands for more proxy information also have been driven in part by these same historical events, since shareholders and investors are more interested than ever in assurances that boards are keeping their fiduciary and governance commitments to company shareholders and stakeholders. This accountability extends to the imposition of some very direct responses to keep boards in line and even includes the potential "claw back" of excess incentive-based compensation given to top company executives. Boards must be more engaged than ever in the company's strategy and the dynamics of the industry in which they compete to understand and respond appropriately to these demands.

Finally, in the coming years boards will see a greater focus on managing both potential financial risk to their company and the external threats posed by cyber criminals. These are such important issues that ISS has stated that it will recommend withholding votes against either the specific committee or the entire board in the event of a significant failure of risk oversight.

WHAT'S NEXT?

The Appendix section of this book contains a host of practical worksheets and assessments that will help the reader implement the recommendations made in this book in order to improve both board governance and productivity.

BOARD OF DIRECTORS ASSESSMENT FORMS

BOARD OF DIRECTORS SELF-ASSESSMENT

Please rank answers to questions from <u>**1 — Strongly Disagree**</u> to <u>**5 — Strongly Agree**</u>

Please include written comments in the space beneath the question or in the space provided at the end of the questionnaire. Your comments are encouraged, as they will be particularly helpful in interpreting the results and in addressing matters not specifically covered by the questions.

I. Questions Relevant to Assessment for the <u>**Company as a Whole**</u>

	Strongly Disagree				Strongly Agree
1. The company will perform well in					
a. the next twelve months.	1	2	3	4	5
b. the next three to five years.	1	2	3	4	5

Comments: _____

_____

_____

	Strongly Disagree				Strongly Agree
2. The company has a compelling strategy that is being implemented effectively.	1	2	3	4	5

Comments: _____

_____

_____

	Strongly Disagree				Strongly Agree
3. The company has the right CEO.	1	2	3	4	5

Comments: _____

_____

_____

	Strongly Disagree				Strongly Agree
4. The company has the right compensation strategy.	1	2	3	4	5

Comments: _____

_____

_____

	Strongly Disagree				Strongly Agree
5. The company has an emergency succession plan in place for its CEO position.	1	2	3	4	5

Comments: _____

_____

_____

	Strongly Disagree				Strongly Agree
6. The company has an appropriate long-term management succession and management development process in place.	1	2	3	4	5

Comments: _____

_____

_____

	Strongly Disagree				Strongly Agree
7. The company has an effective company risk management process in place.	1	2	3	4	5

Comments: _____

_____

_____

II. Questions Relevant to Assessment for the **Board as a Whole**

	Strongly Disagree				Strongly Agree
8. The information that the board receives for board meetings is					
a. useful.	1	2	3	4	5
b. adequate.	1	2	3	4	5
c. in an efficient format.	1	2	3	4	5
d. sufficiently related to the external environment.	1	2	3	4	5
e. timely.	1	2	3	4	5

Comments: _____

_____

_____

	Strongly Disagree				Strongly Agree
9. In general, the board spends about the right amount of time during its meetings discussing each of the following:					
a. strategy	1	2	3	4	5
b. operations	1	2	3	4	5
c. financial results	1	2	3	4	5
d. shareholder issues	1	2	3	4	5
e. organizational issues and succession planning	1	2	3	4	5

Comments: _____
_____
_____

	Strongly Disagree				Strongly Agree
10. The number of meetings per year is appropriate.	1	2	3	4	5

Comments: _____
_____
_____

	Strongly Disagree				Strongly Agree
11. The schedule for each board meeting is satisfactory.	1	2	3	4	5

Comments: _____
_____
_____

	Strongly Disagree				Strongly Agree
12. The board has the right number of directors.	1	2	3	4	5

Comments: _____
_____
_____

	Strongly Disagree				Strongly Agree
13. Individual directors and the board as a whole possess the right skills and backgrounds.	1	2	3	4	5

Comments: _____
_____
_____

	Strongly Disagree				Strongly Agree
14. The process for selection of new board members is satisfactory.	1	2	3	4	5

Comments: _____
_____
_____

	Strongly Disagree				Strongly Agree
15. The compensation for serving as a director is appropriate.	1	2	3	4	5

Comments: _____
_____
_____

	Strongly Disagree				Strongly Agree
16. The board has adequate opportunities to meet with the CEO without other management being present.	1	2	3	4	5

Comments: _____
_____
_____

	Strongly Disagree				Strongly Agree
17. The board has adequate access to members of the company's upper management.	1	2	3	4	5

Comments: _____
_____
_____

	Strongly Disagree				Strongly Agree
18. The board openly communicates its goals, expectations, and concerns to the CEO.	1	2	3	4	5

Comments: _____
_____
_____

	Strongly Disagree				Strongly Agree
19. The board's process for evaluating the CEO is appropriate.	1	2	3	4	5

Comments: _____
_____
_____

	Strongly Disagree				Strongly Agree
20. The leadership of the independent directors is effective.	1	2	3	4	5

Comments: _____
_____
_____

	Strongly Disagree				Strongly Agree
21. Board members are adequately prepared for board meetings.	1	2	3	4	5

Comments: _____
_____
_____

	Strongly Disagree				Strongly Agree
22. Directors are given adequate opportunity for continuing education and for expanding their relevant skills.	1	2	3	4	5

Comments: _____
_____
_____

III. Questions Relevant to Assessment of **Board Group Dynamics**

	Strongly Disagree				Strongly Agree
23. The board's dialogue is of high quality.	1	2	3	4	5

Comments: _____
_____
_____

	Strongly Disagree				Strongly Agree
24. All board members actively participate.	1	2	3	4	5

Comments: _____
_____
_____

	Strongly Disagree				Strongly Agree
25. Board members take reasoned, independent positions.	1	2	3	4	5

Comments: _____
_____
_____

	Strongly Disagree				Strongly Agree
26. Some board members tend to drift off topic.	1	2	3	4	5

Comments: _____
_____
_____

	Strongly Disagree				Strongly Agree
27. The board is unrealistically optimistic about its future.	1	2	3	4	5

Comments: _____
_____
_____

	Strongly Disagree				Strongly Agree
28. The board is more concerned about maintaining harmony than having uncomfortable conversations.	1	2	3	4	5

Comments: _____
_____
_____

	Strongly Disagree				Strongly Agree
29. Board members are sometimes unable to manage our time effectively.	1	2	3	4	5

Comments: _____
_____
_____

	Strongly Disagree				Strongly Agree
30. Board discussions are open and candid.	1	2	3	4	5

Comments: _____
_____
_____

	Strongly Disagree				Strongly Agree
31. Board members listen to and consider each other's comments.	1	2	3	4	5

Comments: _____

_____

_____

	Strongly Disagree				Strongly Agree
32. The atmosphere of the boardroom encourages critical thinking.	1	2	3	4	5

Comments: _____

_____

_____

	Strongly Disagree				Strongly Agree
33. The board relies too much on the opinions of one or two members.	1	2	3	4	5

Comments: _____

_____

_____

	Strongly Disagree				Strongly Agree
34. Sometimes the board delays dealing with difficult issues.	1	2	3	4	5

Comments: _____
_____
_____

35. The top three priorities for the board for the next year are
a. _____
b. _____
c. _____

Comments: _____
_____
_____

Please include any other comments or suggestions on the effectiveness of the board as a whole, or on the performance or effectiveness of any individual director, if desired.

_____
_____
_____
_____
_____
_____
_____
_____
_____
_____

The Board Culture Profile Scoring Legend

The Board Culture Profile is embedded in the larger Board of Directors Self-Assessment (Appendix A). It is designated as Section III. Board Group Dynamics and represents questions #23–34. There are 12 questions in total for this section, three for each culture type scale. Please note that questions #24, #30, and #32 are reversed scored in the following way:

Strongly Agree   = 1 (instead of 5)
Agree   = 2 (instead of 4)
Neither   = 3 (remains the same)
Disagree   = 4 (instead of 2)
Strongly Disagree   = 5 (instead of 1)

Board Culture	Questions to be Scored	Total Score by Culture Type
Detached	#24 (R) __ #26 __ #34 __	TOTAL SCORE:
Dramatic	#27 __ #28 __ #30 (R) __	TOTAL SCORE:
Dependent	#29 __ #32 (R) __ #33 __	TOTAL SCORE:
Dynamic	#23 __ #25 __ #31 __	TOTAL SCORE:

Normed Percentages for the Culture Type Scores:

Detached   5–10% Higher scores indicate that *Groupthink* is more likely to occur.
Dramatic   5–10% Higher scores indicate that *The Abilene Paradox* is more likely to occur.
Dependent   15–20% Higher scores indicate that either *Groupthink* or *The Abilene Paradox* is more likely to occur.
Dynamic   60% or greater Scores less than this indicate a lower level of board culture.

AUDIT COMMITTEE ASSESSMENT

(Please indicate if you are the committee chairman.)
Please rank answers to questions from 1—**Strongly Disagree** to
5—**Strongly Agree**

	Strongly Disagree				Strongly Agree
1. This committee is effective.	1	2	3	4	5
2. The output of the committee is supporting the full board.	1	2	3	4	5
3. The committee confronts the right issues.	1	2	3	4	5
4. The committee gives the CEO candid, decisive feedback.	1	2	3	4	5
5. The committee is able to make collective judgments about important matters.	1	2	3	4	5

(continued)

	Strongly Disagree				Strongly Agree
6. The committee has laid out a full-year agenda.	1	2	3	4	5
7. The committee's composition is appropriate.	1	2	3	4	5
8. The leadership of the committee is effective.	1	2	3	4	5
9. The committee chairperson elicits contributions from all members.	1	2	3	4	5
10. The committee allocates the right amount of time for its work.	1	2	3	4	5

Comments: _____

_____

_____

_____

_____

COMPENSATION COMMITTEE ASSESSMENT

(Please indicate if you are the committee chairman.)
Please rank answers to questions from <u>1 — Strongly Disagree</u> to
<u>5 — Strongly Agree</u>

	Strongly Disagree				Strongly Agree
1. This committee is effective.	1	2	3	4	5
2. The output of the committee is supporting the full board.	1	2	3	4	5
3. The committee confronts the right issues.	1	2	3	4	5
4. The committee gives the CEO candid, decisive feedback.	1	2	3	4	5
5. The committee is able to make collective judgments about important matters.	1	2	3	4	5

(continued)

	Strongly Disagree				Strongly Agree
6. The committee has laid out a full-year agenda.	1	2	3	4	5
7. The committee's composition is appropriate.	1	2	3	4	5
8. The leadership of the committee is effective.	1	2	3	4	5
9. The committee chairperson elicits contributions from all members.	1	2	3	4	5
10. The committee allocates the right amount of time for its work.	1	2	3	4	5

Comments: _____

_____

_____

_____

_____

GOVERNANCE/ NOMINATING COMMITTEE ASSESSMENT

(Please indicate if you are the committee chairman.)
Please rank answers to questions from <u>1—Strongly Disagree</u> to
<u>5—Strongly Agree</u>

	Strongly Disagree				Strongly Agree
1. This committee is effective.	1	2	3	4	5
2. The output of the committee is supporting the full board.	1	2	3	4	5
3. The committee confronts the right issues.	1	2	3	4	5
4. The committee gives the CEO candid, decisive feedback.	1	2	3	4	5

(continued)

	Strongly Disagree				Strongly Agree
5. The committee is able to make collective judgments about important matters.	1	2	3	4	5
6. The committee has laid out a full-year agenda.	1	2	3	4	5
7. The committee's composition is appropriate.	1	2	3	4	5
8. The leadership of the committee is effective.	1	2	3	4	5
9. The committee chairperson elicits contributions from all members.	1	2	3	4	5
10. The committee allocates the right amount of time for its work.	1	2	3	4	5

Comments: _____

_____

_____

_____

_____

CEO ASSESSMENT

Please rank answers to questions from **1—Strongly Disagree** to **5—Strongly Agree**

Please include written comments in the space beneath the question or in the space provided at the end of the questionnaire. Your comments are encouraged, as they will be particularly helpful in interpreting the results and in addressing matters not specifically covered by the questions.

	Strongly Disagree				Strongly Agree
1. The company has performed well over the past twelve months	1	2	3	4	5

Comments: _____

_____

_____

	Strongly Disagree				Strongly Agree
2. The company will perform well in					
a. the next twelve months.	1	2	3	4	5
b. the next three to five years.	1	2	3	4	5

Comments: _____
_____
_____

	Strongly Disagree				Strongly Agree
3. The CEO has made appropriately balanced short-term and long-term decisions.	1	2	3	4	5

Comments: _____
_____
_____

	Strongly Disagree				Strongly Agree
4. The company has a competitive advantage.	1	2	3	4	5

Comments: _____
_____
_____

	Strongly Disagree				Strongly Agree
5. The CEO has developed a compelling strategy.	1	2	3	4	5

Comments: _____
_____
_____

	Strongly Disagree				Strongly Agree
6. The CEO is effectively executing the strategy.	1	2	3	4	5

Comments: _____
_____
_____

	Strongly Disagree				Strongly Agree
7. The CEO has a team that is of consistently high quality.	1	2	3	4	5

Comments: _____
_____
_____

	Strongly Disagree				Strongly Agree
8. The pipeline of leaders ensures continuity for the future.	1	2	3	4	5

Comments: _____
_____
_____

	Strongly Disagree				Strongly Agree
9. The management team is properly focused.	1	2	3	4	5

Comments: _____
_____
_____

	Strongly Disagree				Strongly Agree
10. The CEO is a good leader regarding					
a. the investment community.	1	2	3	4	5
b. shareholders.	1	2	3	4	5

(continued)

	Strongly Disagree				Strongly Agree
c. regulators.	1	2	3	4	5
d. the community at large.	1	2	3	4	5

Comments: _____
_____
_____

11. What advice would you give the CEO?

_____
_____
_____

Comments: _____
_____
_____

LEAD DIRECTOR ASSESSMENT

Please rank answers to questions from 1—Strongly Disagree to 5—Strongly Agree

The lead director _____

	Strongly Disagree				Strongly Agree
1. Is effective.	1	2	3	4	5
2. Effectively organizes, sets the agenda for, and leads executive sessions of, the independent directors.	1	2	3	4	5
3. Serves effectively as a liaison between the board and the Chairman/CEO.	1	2	3	4	5

(continued)

	Strongly Disagree				Strongly Agree
4. Consults with the Chairman/CEO and secretary to set the agenda for board meetings.	1	2	3	4	5
5. Meets with the Chairman/ CEO between board meetings as appropriate in order to facilitate board meetings and discussions.	1	2	3	4	5

6. What advice would you give the lead director?

_____
_____
_____
_____

Other Comments: _____

_____
_____
_____
_____

NONEXECUTIVE CHAIRMAN ASSESSMENT

Please rank answers to questions from <u>1—Strongly Disagree</u> to <u>5—Strongly Agree</u>

	Strongly Disagree				Strongly Agree
1. Provides leadership to the board of directors.	1	2	3	4	5
2. Effectively organizes, sets the agenda for, and leads executive sessions of the independent directors.	1	2	3	4	5
3. Serves effectively as a liaison between the board and the CEO.	1	2	3	4	5
4. Consults with the CEO and secretary to set the agenda for board meetings.	1	2	3	4	5

(continued)

	Strongly Disagree				Strongly Agree
5. Meets with the CEO between board meetings as appropriate in order to facilitate board meetings and discussions.	1	2	3	4	5

6. What advice would you give the chairman?

_____

_____

_____

_____

Other Comments: _____

_____

_____

_____

_____

_____

PEER ASSESSMENT

Please complete this survey by indicating your rating of each director. Please include written comments in the space provided at the end of the questionnaire. Your comments will be particularly helpful for addressing matters not specifically covered by the questions.

Unacceptable = 1; Below Average = 2; Satisfactory = 3; Above Average = 4; Excellent = 5

	Director 1	Director 2	Director 3	Director 4	Director 5	Director 6	Director 7
1. Regularly attends all board meetings							
2. Comes to board meetings well prepared							
3. Participates in a constructive and effective manner, contributing to discussions without dominating them							
4. Communicates with candor and tact, helping the board to manage conflict constructively							

(continued)

	Director 1	Director 2	Director 3	Director 4	Director 5	Director 6	Director 7
5. Exercises independence of judgment when considering issues, even if taking an unpopular position on an issue							
6. Encourages other directors to contribute to board discussions, and listens to and respects the opinions of others							
7. Makes an effort to know and interact with members of management and fellow board members							
8. Asks questions that are focused on policy and strategy rather than on tactics and details							
9. Gets to the heart of a discussion quickly							
10. Would recommend that this director serves another term on the board							
Average Score							

NOTES

PREFACE

1. Sparks, William, "Group Culture Assessment Scale" (PhD diss., The George Washington University, 2002).

CHAPTER 1

1. Carola Frydman and Raven E. Saks, "Historical Trends in Executive Compensation, 1936–2003" (working paper, Massachusetts Institute of Technology, 2007), 7. Retrieved from www.vanderbilt.edu/econ/sempapers/Frydman1.pdf.

2. Malcolm Gladwell, *Outliers: The Story of Success* (New York: Penguin, 2009), 128.

3. Walter Kiechel, *The Lords of Strategy: The Secret Intellectual History of the New Corporate World* (Boston, Harvard Business School Press, 2010), 10.

4. Jerry Z. Muller, "Capitalism and Inequality: What the Right and the Left Get Wrong," *Foreign Affairs*, March/April 2013, 42–43.

5. Frydman and Saks, "Historical Trends," 9.

6. Graef Crystal, *In Search of Excess: The Overcompensation of American Executives* (New York, NY: Ecco Press, 1991), 10.

7. Mark Maremont and Charles Forelle, "Bosses' Pay: How Stock Options Became Part of the Problem," *Wall Street Journal*, December 27, 2006, 4.

8. Frydman and Saks, "Historical Trends," 8.

9. Robert D. Hershey Jr., "A Little Industry with a Lot of Sway on Proxy Votes," *New York Times*, June 16, 2006, 1.

10. Hersey, "A Little Industry."

11. Securities and Exchange Commission, "Proxy Voting: Proxy Voting Responsibilities of Investment Advisers and Availability of Exemptions from the Proxy Rules for Proxy Advisory Firms," June 30, 2014. Accessed August 1, 2015, www.sec.gov/interps/legal/cfslb20.htm.

12. Lindsay Frost, "Activist Campaigns See Mixed Results in Proxy Votes," *Agenda*, published by *Money-Media*, May 15, 2015.

13. Emily Lambert, "The Right Way to Pay," *Forbes*, May 11, 2009. Accessed August 1, 2015, www.forbes.com/forbes/2009/0511/078-executives-compensation-business-right-way-to-pay.html.

14. David Gelles, "It's Still Their Party," *New York Times*, May 17, 2015, 2. Accessed August 3, 2015, www.nytimes.com/2015/05/17/business/for-the-highest-paid-ceos-the-party-goes-on.html.

CHAPTER 2

1. Home Depot. "Our History." Accessed June 1, 2015, https://corporate.homedepot.com/ourcompany/history/pages/default.aspx.

2. Parija Bhatnagar, "Shareholders to Home Depot Chief: You're Chicken," CNN Money, May 26, 2006. Accessed August 1, 2015, http://money.cnn.com/2006/05/25/news/companies/home_depot.

3. David H. Langstaff, "Rethinking Shareholder Value and the Purpose of the Corporation" (speech presented at the Kellogg School of Management–Northwestern University Aspen Institute Business and Society Program, March 7–8, 2013).

4. Schumpeter, "The Business of Business," An Old Debate about What Companies Are for Has Been Revived, *Economist*, March 21, 2015. Accessed July 31, 2015, www.economist.com/

news/business/21646742-old-debate-about-what-companies-are-has-been-revived-business-business.

5. Letter by Laurence D. Fink, Chairman and CEO of Black-Rock, to five hundred companies in the United States, March 31, 2015.

6. William Shakespeare, *Henry IV, Part I*, Act 3, Scene 1, 52–58.

7. Peter F. Drucker, "What Makes an Effective Manager," *Harvard Business Review*, June 2004, 59.

8. Matthew J. Paese, "Your Next CEO: Why Succession Planning Is More Important Than Ever," *Conference Board Review*, October 11, 2001, 19.

9. David F. Larcker and Brian Tayan, "Leadership Challenges at Hewlett-Packard: Through the Looking Glass," *Stanford Closer Look Series*, 2011.

10. Larcker and Tayan, "Leadership Challenges at Hewlett-Packard."

11. Eric Jackson, "Six Years Later—The Problem at HP Is Still the Board," *Forbes* (blog), January 16, 2012. Accessed August 1, 2015, www.forbes.com/sites/ericjackson/2012/01/16/six-years-later-the-problem-at-hp-is-still-the-board.

CHAPTER 3

1. Alan Greenspan, "The Challenge of Central Banking in a Democratic Society" (comment made during a televised speech at The American Enterprise Institute for Public Policy Research in Washington, DC, December 5, 1996), www.federalreserve.gov/boarddocs/speeches/1996/19961205.htm.

2. National Public Radio, "The Fall of Enron." Accessed July 29, 2015, www.npr.org/news/specials/enron.

3. Simon Romero and Riva D. Atlas, "WorldCom Files for Bankruptcy—Largest U.S. Case," *New York Times*, July 22, 2002. Accessed July 29, 2015, www.nytimes.com/2002/07/

22/us/worldcom-s-collapse-the-overview-worldcom-files-for-bankruptcy-largest-us-case.html.

4. Public Company Accounting Oversight Board. "PCAOB Over-sees the Auditors of Companies to Protect Investors." Accessed July 29, 2015, http://pcaobus.org/Pages/default.aspx.

5. Andreas Cremer and Ilona Wissenbach, "VW Struggles in 'Diplomacy Phase' as Investors Weigh CEO Change," Reuters, April 15, 2015. Accessed July 29, 2015, www.reuters.com/article/2015/04/15/volkswagen-ceo-succession-idUSL5N0XC1DG20150415.

6. Letter dated September 20, 2012 by Christine Shaw, Deputy Treasurer, State of Connecticut, on behalf of the Connecticut Retirement Plans and Trust Fund (CRPTF) to Alan Braver-man, Secretary, The Walt Disney company.

7. 2014 Board Index report, Spencer Stuart, Inc. Accessed July 29, 2015, www.spencerstuart.com/~/media/PDF%20Files/Research%20and%20Insight%20PDFs/SSBI2014web14Nov2014.pdf.

8. David F. Larcker and Brian Tayan, "Where Experts Get It Wrong: Independence vs. Leadership in Corporate Govern-ance" (Working Paper No. 3196, Stanford Closer Look Series, March 14, 2014. Accessed July 29, 2015, www.gsb.stanford.edu/faculty-research/working-papers/where-experts-get-it-wrong-independence-vs-leadership-corporate.

9. BlackRock, "Proxy Voting Guidelines for U. S. Securities," February 2015. Accessed July 29, 2015, www.blackrock.com/corporate/en-us/literature/fact-sheet/blk-responsible-investment-guidelines-us.pdf.

10. 2014 Board Index report, Spencer Stuart, Inc.

11. Quentin Hardyman, "John Chambers Steps Aside at Cisco as Generational Shift Arrives," New York Times, May 4, 2015. Accessed August 1, 2015, www.nytimes.com/2015/05/05/technology/cisco-names-charles-robbins-to-succeed-ceo-john-chambers.html.

12. Lowes.com. "Governance Guidelines." Accessed August 3, 2015, http://phx.corporate-ir.net/phoenix.zhtml?c=95223&p=irol-govguidelines.

13. Nucor.com. "Governance Principles." Accessed August 3, 2015, www.nucor.com/governance/principles.

14. Letter by William NcNabb, CEO of Vanguard, to corporations, February 2015.

15. Letter by Larry Fink, Chairman and CEO of BlackRock, to corporations, March 3, 2015.

CHAPTER 4

1. Elliott Jaques, *The Changing Culture of a Factory* (London: Tavistock, 1951), p. 3.

2. Edgar H. Schein, *Leadership and Organizational Culture* (San Francisco: Jossey-Bass, 1985), p. 5.

3. Daniel F. Forbes and Francis J. Milliken, "Cognition and Corporate Governance: Understanding Boards of Directors as Strategic Decision-Making Groups," *Academy of Management Review* 24 (1999): 489–505.

4. Jeffrey A. Sonnenfeld, "What Makes Great Boards Great," *Harvard Business Review*, September 2002.

5. Kathleen Eisenhardt, Jean Kahwajy, and L. J. Bourgeois, "How Management Teams Can Have a Good Fight," *Harvard Business Review*, July–August 1997.

6. Solange Charas, "The Impact of Board Dynamics on Shareholder Value Creation." *Director Notes*, The Conference Board, February 2014: 1–8.

7. Timothy A. Judge, Chad A. Higgins, Carl J. Thoresen, and Murray R. Barrick, "The Big Five Personality Traits, General Mental Ability, and Career Success across the Life Span," *Personnel Psychology* 52, no. 3 (1999): 561–840.

8. Michael Maccoby, "Narcissistic Leaders: The Incredible Pros, the Inevitable Cons," *Harvard Business Review*, January–February 2004, pp 1–11.

9. Pamela Davies, personal communication, May 14, 2015.

10. Pamela Davies, personal communication, May 14, 2015.

11. Sue Shellenbarger, "What Corporate Climbers Can Teach Us," *Wall Street Journal*, July 14, 2014.

12. David Larcker and Brian Tayan. "Where Experts Get It Wrong: Independence vs. Leadership in Corporate Governance," *Stanford Closer Look Series*, March 14, 2013, http://www.gsb.stanford.edu/faculty-research/working-papers/where-experts-get-it-wrong-independence-vs-leadership-corporate.

13. Larcker and Tayan, "Where Experts Get It Wrong."

14. Lead Director Network ViewPoints, December 1, 2010. Issue 9, 1–12.

15. W. L. Sparks, "Group Culture and Basic Assumption Mental States: The Design, Development and Validation of an Attitude Assessment Scale" (unpublished doctoral dissertation, Washington, DC: George Washington University, 2002).

16. Sparks, "Group Culture and Basic Assumption Mental States."

17. Sonnenfeld, "What Makes Great Boards Great."

CHAPTER 5

1. Emile Durkheim, *The Division of Labor in Society* (New York: Macmillan, 1933), 19.

2. Sigmund Freud, *Group Psychology and the Analysis of the Ego*, trans. J. Strachey (New York: W. W. Norton & Company, Inc., 1950), 11.

3. Gustave Le Bon, *The Crowd* (London: Benn, 1947; reprint, New York: Viking Press, 1960), 18 (page citation is to the reprint edition).

4. Solomon Asch, *Social Psychology* (Englewood Cliffs, NJ: Prentice-Hall, 1952).

5. Cass R. Sunstein and Reid Hastie, *Wiser: Getting Beyond Groupthink to Make Groups Smarter* (Boston: Harvard Business Review Press, 2015).

6. Irving L. Janis, *Groupthink: Psychological Studies of Policy Decisions and Fiascoes*, 2nd ed. (Boston: Wadsworth, Cengage Learning, 1982).

7. Jerry B. Harvey, *The Abilene Paradox and Other Meditations on Management* (San Francisco: Jossey-Bass, 1988).

8. Janis, *Groupthink*.

9. Harvey, *The Abilene Paradox*.

CHAPTER 6

1. David F. Larcker and Brian Tayan, "Where Experts Get It Wrong: Independence vs. Leadership in Corporate Governance," *Stanford Closer Look Series*, March 14, 2013, http://www.gsb.stanford.edu/faculty-research/working-papers/where-experts-get-it-wrong-independence-vs-leadership-corporate.

2. 2014 Board Index, Spencer Stuart, Inc. Accessed July 29, 2015, www.spencerstuart.com/~/media/PDF%20Files/Research%20and%20Insight%20PDFs/SSBI2014web14Nov2014.pdf.

3. 2014 Board Index, Spencer Stuart, Inc.

4. 2014 Board Index, Spencer Stuart, Inc.

CHAPTER 7

1. NYSE Listed Company Manual, 2002. Accessed August 1, 2015, http://nysemanual.nyse.com/LCMTools/PlatformViewer.asp?selectednode=chp_1_4_3_10&manual=%2Flcm%2Fsections%2Flcm-sections%2F.

2. Nucor.com. "Governance Principles." Accessed August 3, 2015, www.nucor.com/governance/principles/index.php?page=6.

3. General Electric.com. "2015 Annual Meeting and Proxy Statement." Accessed August 3, 2015, www.ge.com/ar2014/assets/pdf/GE_2015_Proxy_Statement.pdf.

4. 2014 Board Index, Spencer Stuart, Inc. Accessed July 29, 2015, www.spencerstuart.com/~/media/PDF%20Files/Research%20and%20Insight%20PDFs/SSBI2014web14Nov2014.pdf.

5. Steven R. Walker, National Association of Board Directors, August 28, 2012.

CHAPTER 8

1. Ram Charan, Dennis Carey, and Michael Useem, *Boards That Lead—When to Take Charge, When to Partner, and When to Lead* (New York, Harvard Business Review Press, 2014).

2. Nucor.com. "Governance Principles." Accessed August 3, 2015, www.nucor.com/governance/principles/index.php?page=6.

CHAPTER 9

1. Rakhi Kumar, "Addressing the Need for Board Refreshment and Director Succession in Investee Companies," State Street Global Advisors, *IQ Insights* (February 15, 2015). Accessed August 2, 2015, www.ssga.com/investment-topics/general-investing/2015/Addressing-the-Need-for-Board%20Refreshment-in-Investee-Companies.pdf.

2. 2015 Board Index, Spencer Stuart, Inc. Accessed July 29, 2015, www.spencerstuart.com/~/media/PDF%20Files/Research%20and%20Insight%20PDFs/SSBI2014web14Nov2014.pdf

3. 2015 Board Index, Spencer Stuart, Inc.

4. BlackRock. "Proxy Voting Guidelines for U.S. Securities," February 2015, www.blackrock.com/corporate/en-us/literature/fact-sheet/blk-responsible-investment-guidelines-us.pdf.

5. 2015 Board Index, Spencer Stuart, Inc.

6. 2015 Board Index, Spencer Stuart, Inc.

7. *Agenda*, a Financial Times Service, "Graying of Corporate Boards Continues" (January 23, 2105), www.agendaweek.com/pc/1050203/108163.

8. Solange Charas, "Improving Corporate Performance by Enhancing Team Dynamics at the Board Level," *International Journal of Disclosure and Governance* (January 9, 2015). Accessed August 2, 2015, http://www.palgrave-journals.com/jdg/journal/v12/n2/full/jdg201335a.html.

CHAPTER 10

1. Marc S. Gerber and Richard J. Grossman, "Proxy Access: The 2015 Proxy Season and Beyond," June 23, 2015. Accessed July 31, 2015, www.skadden.com/insights/proxy-access-2015-proxy-season-and-beyond.

2. *Agenda*, A *Financial Times Service*, "Calpers Cautions on Composition Policy" (July 10, 2015), p 16.

ABOUT THE AUTHORS

PETER C. BROWNING

As founder and managing Director of Peter Browning Partners, LLC, a board advisory service, Peter Browning has a wide range of experience in business. Beginning as a sales trainee, he spent twenty-four years with the Continental Can Company, including being President of two different divisions, last serving as Executive Vice President–Operating Officer. He joined National Gypsum Company in 1989, and in September 1990, he was elected Chairman, President, and Chief Executive Officer of National Gypsum Company, seeing the company through and out of bankruptcy.

He joined Sonoco Products Company (a $5 billion global packaging company) in November 1993, where he last served as President and Chief Executive Officer before retiring in July 2000. In March 2002 he was appointed Dean of the McColl School of Business at Queens University of Charlotte, North Carolina, where he served until May 2005.

He is a native of Boston, Massachusetts. A 1963 graduate of Colgate University with an AB in history, he earned his MBA from the University of Chicago in 1976. The Harvard Business School prepared a case study regarding his success in effecting changes at Continental's White Cap Division. A case study has also been written on his experience at National Gypsum for use at the University of North Carolina Kenan–Flagler Business School.

Since 1989 he has served on the board of directors of thirteen publicly traded companies, including ten years at Wachovia Corporation and sixteen years at Lowes Companies. During that time he has been Chairman and CEO, CEO, nonexecutive chair, lead director, and chair of audit, compensation, and governance/nominating committees. Browning is currently the lead director of Acuity Brands and a member of the board of directors of ScanSource, Inc. In 2015 he retired from the board of EnPro Industries, Inc. and from Nucor Corporation, where he served six years as nonexecutive chair and as lead director for six years. In January 2013 he joined the board of Equilar, the leading provider of compensation and governance data, as lead independent director.

In the fall of 2004, *Board Alert Magazine* selected Browning as one of eight "Outstanding Directors of the Year" for his role in the successful CEO transitions at Lowe's and Nucor. He is also the 2009 recipient of Boston University's "Gislason Award for Leadership in Executive Development." He was selected for the "2011 and 2012 NACD Director 100 List" (the list of the most influential people in corporate governance in the boardroom).

The Nucor Corporation 2014 Annual Report noted: "This year also marks Peter Browning's final year on the board of directors. I cannot say enough about the tremendous value Peter brought to Nucor during his 15 years as a director . . . . Peter sets the standard by which other public company directors are measured. His knowledge of corporate governance, outstanding judgment and excellent interpersonal skills are second to none . . . ."

In April 2010 his chapter, "Leadership in the Corner Office: The Board's Most Important Responsibility," was published in a book by Jossey-Bass and the Center for Creative Leadership titled *Extraordinary Leadership: Addressing the Gaps in Senior Executive Development*.

In addition, Peter is a founding member of the Lead Director Network and a frequent participant in governance seminars, serving on panels addressing a wide variety of corporate governance and compensation issues.

He is a lifetime member of The University of Chicago, Council on the Booth Graduate School of Business, and he served on the Executive Committee of the National Association of Manufacturers.

WILLIAM L. SPARKS, PhD

William Sparks is Vice President of Talent with EnPro Industries, a $1.5 billion global manufacturing company headquartered in Charlotte, North Carolina. In this role he is responsible for the leadership development, learning, and talent initiatives across the company. He is a Managing Partner with Peter Browning Partners, LLC. Concurrently, he serves as the Dennis Thompson Chair of Leadership at the McColl School of Business at Queens University of Charlotte, North Carolina, where he is tenured Professor of Business and Behavioral Sciences. He also serves as Visiting Professor of Management with Franklin University in Lugano, Switzerland. He received the Fuqua Distinguished Educator Award for excellence in teaching at Queens in 2003 and 2005, and he was awarded the inaugural McColl School Leadership in Teaching Award in 2009.

He holds a BA in Psychology and Philosophy/Religion from Winthrop University and an MA in Industrial/Organizational Psychology and Human Resource Management from Appalachian State University. He completed his PhD in Organizational Behavior and Development from The George Washington University's School of Business and Public Management, where his research focused on group dynamics, organizational culture, and leadership.

INDEX

Note: Page references in *italics* refer to figures.